Teedląy t'iin naholndak niign

Stories by the Tetlin People

Told by
Cora David
in her native Athabascan language

Edited by
Olga Lovick

Alaska Native Language Center
University of Alaska Fairbanks
2011

First Edition

First Printing 2011

Second Printing 2012

Printed in the United States of America.

Library of Congress Cataloging-in-Publication Data

David, Cora, 1935-

Teedlay t'iin naholndak niign : stories by the Tetlin people / told by Cora David, edited by Olga Lovick. -- 1st ed.

p. cm.

Includes bibliographical references.

ISBN-13: 978-1-55500-114-8

ISBN-10: 1-55500-114-9

1. Tanana Indians--Alaska--Tetlin--History. 2. Tanana Indians--Alaska--Tetlin--Social life and customs. 3. Upper Tanana language--Dialects--Alaska--Tetlin--Texts. 4. Upper Tanana language--Dialects--Alaska--Tetlin--Translating into English. 5. Tetlin (Alaska)--History. 6. Tetlin (Alaska)--Social life and customs. I. Lovick, Olga Charlotte. II. Title.

E99.T187D38 2011

979.8'6--dc23

2011025219

Front cover photo of Porcupine Grass Mountain © Jessica Cherry and Forest Kirst.

Back cover photo of Cora David by Siri Tuttle.

Address correspondence to:

Alaska Native Language Center

PO Box 757680

Fairbanks, AK 99775-7680

rafroese@alaska.edu

Teedlą̨y t'iin naholndak niign

Stories by the Tetlin People

Ay jah dinahtl'aa k'it nahogndagn
shnaa ch'ale hǫshdiinitniign ch'a nahogndagn
ay ha ukol t'oot'eey ay ch'ale.

What I said for this book here,
what I told here, my mother told me
and nothing else.

Contents

Part I

Nidhihshyąą niign
Stories of how I grew up

Part II

Łąy eł t'eey hutshyaak niign
Stories that really happened

Part III

Ts'exuushyąąk niign
Stories how we can become smart

About This Collection

By Olga Lovick

This is a collection of narratives told by Tetlin Elder Cora David in her Native language, the Tetlin dialect of Upper Tanana Athabascan. Upper Tanana was formerly spoken in five settlements in Alaska and the Yukon Territory: (from west to east) Tetlin, Nabesna, Northway, Scottie Creek, and Beaver Creek. Today, most speakers live in Tetlin, Northway, and Beaver Creek or have left the Upper Tanana area altogether. There are fewer than 100 speakers now, and most of them are in their 50s or older.

Cora David, born in 1935, is one of the last few fluent speakers of the Tetlin dialect. She grew up in *Nahk'ade* ('fishing place', Last Tetlin) with her parents and siblings. Her family had a semi-nomadic lifestyle. During the summers, the family went to their camp in Nahk'ade to catch whitefish. Cora's father, Alfred Adam, also had a large garden, which

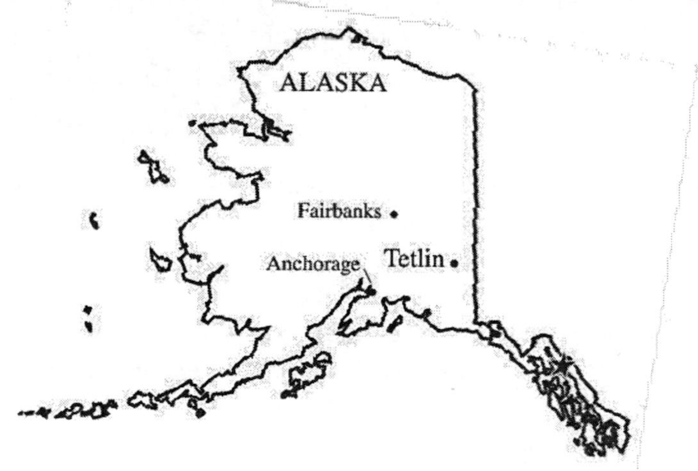

provided the family with vegetables. During the fall and winter, the family moved around, harvesting different resources. Cora also attended the school in Tetlin. Later, Cora left Tetlin for a few years to work in Anchorage. She returned to Tetlin in 1967 and married Roy David in 1969. They have lived in Tetlin since. She has taught the language and culture at the local school and is a renowned storyteller and singer in the Upper Tanana area.

Cora remembers how her mother, Lucy, would always tell the children stories at bedtime. Sometimes, Lucy would tell them stories all night long. Lucy did not speak any English and spoke only her language to her children.

This collection is organized into three parts. The first part (*Nidhihshyąą niign* 'Stories of how I grew up') describes events that happened during Cora's lifetime and that she remembers herself. The stories are organized chronologically, starting with the most recent one (in the 1970s) and ending in her childhood memories. Several of these stories describe the migratory way of life of an old-time Athabascan family.

Lucy Adam on her 105th birthday. Photo © Sam Harrel, *Fairbanks Daily News-Miner*

The second part (*Łąy eł t'eey hutshyaak niign* 'Stories that really happened') describes events that Cora herself has not witnessed but that she learned from her mother, Lucy. The first three of these take place during the lifetime of Cora's mother, while the other three are set further back in time. All of these are true stories.

The third part (*Ts'exuushyąąk niign* 'Stories how we can become smart') contains old-time stories. Cora says they are like fairy tales in that we do not know if things really happened that way, but they teach

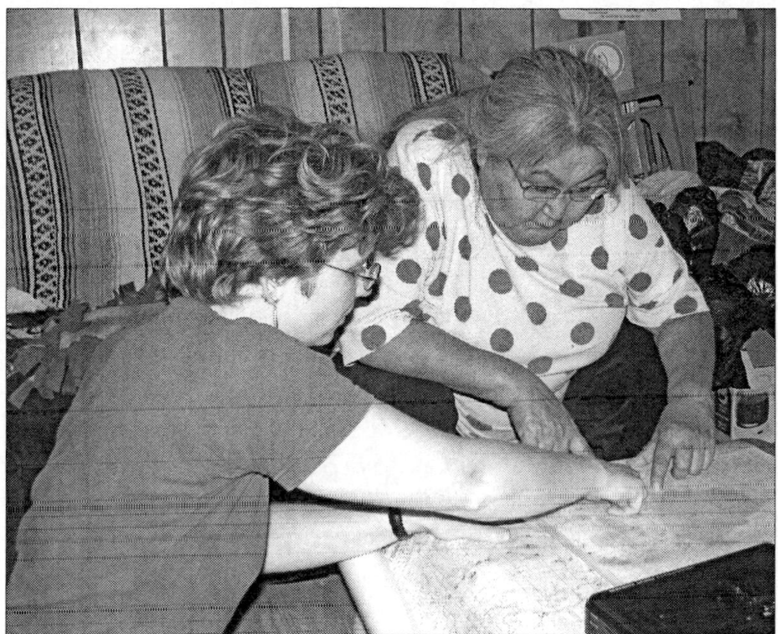

Olga Lovick and Cora David. Photo © Siri Tuttle, 2009.

us about proper behavior and explain why the world is the way it is. The story of Nedzeegn teaches us about respect and kindness. The next three stories are part of the Yamaagn Teeshyay ("the man who went around the world") story cycle. This is an important story cycle in many Alaskan Athabascan groups. The last story in this collection, *Stsǫǫ Kelahdzeey xa nahoholndag* 'The story they tell about Grandmother Spider', is an Upper Tanana classic and explains, among other things, why killing a spider causes rain!

I first met Cora in December 2006, and we became friends quickly. Her enthusiasm for and skill in telling stories became apparent very soon, and the collection grew rapidly. A small grant from the Jacobs Fund made it possible for me to return to Alaska in summer 2009 to focus on the transcription and translation of the narratives. All stories were recorded by me between 2007 and 2009. Some of them were recorded in Cora's home in Tetlin, some in my home in Fairbanks, and some in various locations in Tok. All of the stories were audio-recorded, and we also have video recordings for some of them. Most of the time, there was no audience other than myself, although sometimes Cora's family members were present. On a few occasions, other linguists (Siri Tuttle, Isabel Nuñez-Ortiz, James Kari) were also present.

We present the stories with the Upper Tanana text on the left page and a line-by-line translation into English on the facing page. The line breaks usually correspond to pause groups, that is, groups of words that are separated by a pause. Punctuation was informed by intonation: when Cora's voice went up at the end of a line, this is indicated by a question mark; when her voice went down, we wrote a period; and a comma indicates steady pitch. Sometimes, she would hold a syllable extra-long for emphasis or effect. This is indicated by colons following the lengthened sound (e.g., *guu::::y* 'little', held extra-long).

We felt that including the audio with the narratives gave us a little more freedom in editing and polishing the texts. Thus, the stories presented in here are not written down exactly as they were told. Occasionally, Cora switched into English when telling a story. During the transcription process, she translated those segments back into Upper Tanana. These back-translations are indicated by <single angle brackets>. In other cases, she rephrased the text during the transcription process or thought of an addition. These changes are marked by <<double angle brackets>>. Omissions from the original recordings are generally not marked.

We hope that that this book can be used by a number of audiences and for a number of purposes. It can be used for teaching and learning the language, whether in the schools, at culture camp, at the University of Alaska Fairbanks campus in Tok, or at home. It can be used by community members to find out more about the old way of living, or to compare Cora's experiences to their own. It is intended as a record of Tetlin language and culture, and as such it can be used by linguists, anthropologists, and anyone else with an interest in these topics.

Acknowledgments

Avis Sam, Roy Sam, and Rosa Brewer helped us with the transcription and translation of the stories. Their work is particularly remarkable because they all speak a different (Northway) dialect than Cora does and had to translate between the dialects as well. They also provided much valuable commentary, which is sometimes included in the footnotes to the text. *Tsin’įį* for their hard work!

We thank Polly Hyslop for introducing us (Cora and Olga) to each other. Without her, this work never would have been begun.

Several linguists have provided moral and logistic support. Siri Tuttle’s help was invaluable, especially in the final stages. We also want to acknowledge Isabel Nuñez-Ortiz and James Kari. We also want to thank Gary Holton for his comments on this collection. Special thanks go to Leon Unruh for readying the collection for publication.

We also want to thank Jessica Cherry and Forest Kirst for taking the aerial photographs of relevant landscape features.

Finally, we want to thank our families for giving us the time and space to complete this project, in particular Roy David, Joe Lovick, and Julius Lovick.

The work on this book was begun during Olga Lovick’s University of Alaska Presidential International Polar Year postdoctoral fellowship, sponsored by a generous grant from Conoco-Phillips and housed at the Alaska Native Language Center. It was completed with funding through a grant by the Jacobs Research Fund. We gratefully acknowledge these organizations.

None of the people or organizations is responsible for any errors of fact or representation in this collection.

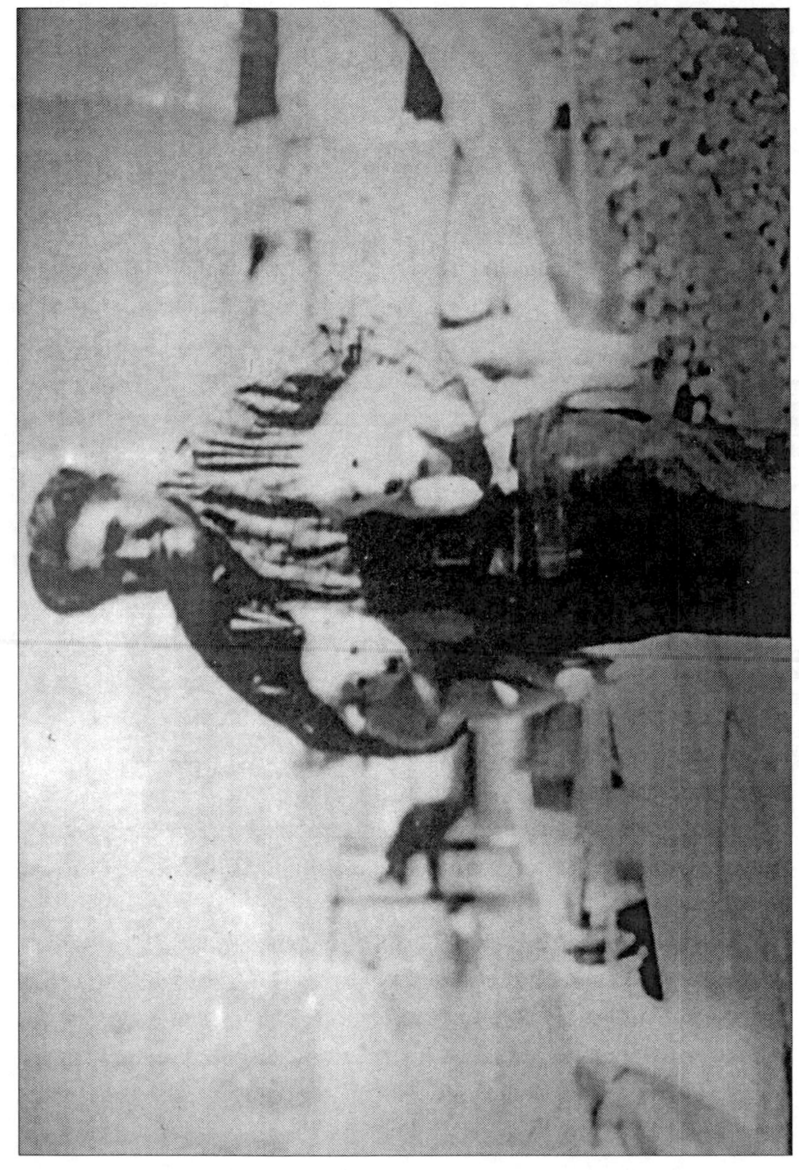

Cora's father, Alfred Adam from Dawson City, Yukon Territory.

The Sounds of Upper Tanana, and How They Are Spelled

By Olga Lovick

Upper Tanana Athabascan contains many sounds that do not exist in English. Other sounds are similar to English ones but are pronounced a little differently. In this section, we discuss the sounds and their spelling.

Trying to accommodate different audiences, we chose two ways of explaining the sounds. For linguists, we include vowel and consonant charts in the hope that they are self-explanatory. For readers with no or little knowledge of linguistics, we include discussions of the sounds and their spelling, comparing them with sounds familiar from English.

Upper Tanana spelling is a lot easier and more consistent than English spelling. Think of how the *ou* is pronounced in the English words *bough, bought, though, rough,* and *through*—five different ways! In Upper Tanana, words are always pronounced the way they are written. Once you have learned how the sounds are written, you can pronounce all Upper Tanana words by looking at how they are written.

Below, we describe all sounds in different ways, but this is not as good as hearing the sounds. For this reason, we recommend that the reader visit www.lithophile.com/olga/ut/alphabet to listen to the sounds of the Upper Tanana alphabet pronounced by several speakers. One of them is Cora David, the narrator of all the stories in this book. The CD included with this book is another way of learning how Upper Tanana sounds.

Some sounds are written by single letters (for example, ***a***, ***m***, ***ł***) and some by combinations of letters (***oo***, ***tth***, ***k'***). Sounds written by letter combinations are still single sounds! In cases where a letter combination actually represents two sounds that happen to occur next to each other, we indicate this by a hyphen. For example, ***k'*** is one sound in the word *k'įįł* 'birch sap', but it is two sounds in the word *nak-'įį* 'I saw'.

Vowels

Vowels are sounds where the flow of air through the mouth is not obstructed in any way and is merely modified by the position of the tongue (high or low, front or back of the mouth) and the rounding of the lips.

Below, we show the vowels of the Tetlin dialect of Upper Tanana. A sound's position in the chart indicates where the tongue is when one pronounces the vowel. If you say "Eeeeeeek!" you'll notice that your tongue is pretty high up and pretty far to the front of your mouth. That is why *i* and *ii* (the Upper Tanana spelling of these sounds) are at the top left of the chart. When you say "Ooooo," your tongue moves to the back of your mouth, but it stays at the top (you'll also notice that your lips are rounded when you say "Ooooo," but not when you say "Eeeeek!") When you say "Aaaaah," your tongue is at the bottom of your mouth. That is why *a* is at the bottom of the chart.

	front		back
top	i ii		u uu
	e ee	ü üü	o oo
bottom		a aa	

Upper Tanana has long and short vowels. Long vowels are written with two vowel symbols ("aa", "uu", and so on), short vowels with one vowel symbol.

aa is pronounced like ***a*** in *father*.

a is pronounced like ***u*** in *duck*.

ee is pronounced like ***a*** in *lazy*, but without the offglide.

e is pronounced like ***e*** in *bet*.

ii is pronounced like ***ee*** in *beetle*.

i is pronounced like ***i*** in *fit*.

oo is pronounced like ***o*** in *bone*, but without the offglide.

o is pronounced like ***o*** in *bone*, but without the offglide, and shorter.

uu is pronounced like ***oo*** in *loon*.

u is pronounced like ***u*** in *butcher*.

üü is pronounced similar to ***ea*** in *learn*, but without the English ***r***. This sound does not exist in English.

ü is pronounced similar to ***ea*** in *learn*, but without the English ***r***, and shorter. This sound does not exist in English.

There is also one diphthong in the Tetlin dialect of Upper Tanana, **ia.** It is pronounced similar to the ***eah*** in *yeah*.

Upper Tanana vowels can be oral or nasal. (English vowels are always oral.) Nasal vowels are pronounced "through the nose." Nasality is indicated through a little hook under the vowel symbol: ąą, ą, ǫǫ, ǫ, and so on.

Consonants

Consonants are sounds made when the flow of air is somehow obstructed. Many Upper Tanana consonants do not exist in English, and many English consonants do not exist in Upper Tanana.

	labial	inter-dental	alveolar	post-alveolar	palatal	velar	glottal
oral stops	mb		d t t’			g k k’	’
affricates		ddh tth tth’	dz ts ts’	j ch ch’			
fricatives		dh th	s	shy sh	yh	x	h
lateral affricates			dl tl tl’				
laterals			l ł				
nasal stops	m		n nh				
glides					y		

The consonants in the following list are not presented in alphabetical order. Instead, similar sounds are grouped together, to make the explanation easier to follow.

’ sounds like the hyphen in the expression *uh-oh*. It is rare in English but frequent in Upper Tanana. This sound is called a “glottal stop”; it is a little catch in the throat.

m is pronounced like English ***m*** in *mother*.

mb is pronounced sometimes like ***mb*** as in *member*, and sometimes like ***b*** as in *bed*. There is no hard and fast rule for when which pronunciation is correct; most speakers vary freely.

n, nd is sometimes pronounced like English ***n*** in *no*, and sometimes like English ***nd*** in *end*. There is no hard and fast rule for determining which pronunciation is correct; most speakers vary freely.

nh is pronounced like English ***n*** in *run*, but without vibration of the vocal cords.

d is pronounced similar English ***d*** in *den*, but without vibration of the vocal cords.

t is pronounced similar to English ***t*** in *ten*.

t' is pronounced similar to English ***t*** in *ten* immediately followed by a glottal stop (see ').

dh is pronounced like English ***th*** in *the* or *this,* never like English ***th*** in *thick* or *through*.

th is pronounced like English ***th*** in *thick* or *through,* never like English ***th*** in *the* or *this*.

ddh is pronounced like English ***t*** followed immediately by ***th*** in *the* or *this*. When you say "a**t th**e edge" quickly, you get something that is very similar to Upper Tanana ***ddh***.

tth is pronounced like English ***t*** followed immediately by ***th*** as in *thick* or *through*. When you say "my righ**t th**umb" quickly, you get something that is very similar to Upper Tanana ***tth***.

tth' is pronounced like Upper Tanana ***tth,*** but followed immediately by a glottal stop (see ').

l is pronounced like English ***l*** in *lot*.

ł is pronounced like English ***l*** in *lot,* but without vibration of the vocal cords. Put the tip of your tongue at your hard palate and let the air come out pretty quickly at the sides of your mouth. There is no identical sound in English, although the ***l*** in *clear* comes close.

dl is pronounced like English ***dl*** in *ladle*.

tl is pronounced like English ***ttl*** in *shuttle* (with a British accent).

tl' is pronounced like English ***ttl*** in *shuttle* (with a British accent) followed by a glottal stop (see ').

s is pronounced like English ***s*** as in *sun*.

dz is pronounced like English ***dz*** in *adze*.

ts is pronounced like English ***ts*** in *fits*.

ts' is pronounced like English ***ts*** in *fits* followed by a glottal stop (see ').

shy is pronounced like English ***sh*** as in *shine* immediately followed by a ***y*** as in *yes*.

sh is pronounced like English ***sh*** as in *shine*.

j is pronounced like English ***j*** in *jeans*.

ch is pronounced like English ***ch*** in *church*.

ch' is pronounced like English ***ch*** in *church* followed by a glottal stop (see ').

y is pronounced like English ***y*** in *yes*.

yh is pronounced like English ***y*** in *yes*, but without vibration of the vocal cords. You make a similar sound if you pronounce the word "tune" carefully: between the *t* and the *u* is a *y*-like sound that is quite similar to Upper Tanana ***yh***.

x is pronounced like ***ch*** in the Scottish word *loch*. This sound does not exist in English.

g is pronounced similar to English ***g*** in *gun*, but without vibration of the vocal cords and a little farther back in the mouth.

k is pronounced similar to English ***c*** in *cook*, but a little farther back in the mouth.

k' is pronounced similar to English ***c*** in *cook*, but a little farther back in the mouth and followed by a glottal stop (see ').

h is pronounced like English ***h*** in *hot*.

Standardization

Some very frequent words have variant forms, e.g. *eh* ~ *eł* 'and, with' or *nts'ą'* ~ *ts'ą'* 'and'. We have standardized the variants to *eł* and *nts'ą'*, respectively.

In the case of other words, we simply wrote the variant that we could hear.

Tone

While some Upper Tanana dialects mark tonal distinctions, the Tetlin dialect exhibits only vestigial tonal contrasts. Hence, tone is not indicated in the transcriptions in this book. The reader interested in tone patterns is encouraged to consult the recordings that accompany this book.

Place Names

Many of Cora’s stories are situated in the Tetlin area and explicitly state where certain events took place. We include a map (on the next page) showing the Tetlin area. On the map, we indicate with a number each of the places mentioned in the stories, plus some that are not mentioned but that are salient when looking at the landscape.

Following is a list of the numbers, the Upper Tanana name of the feature, a literal translation (usually obtained from Cora and verified using Kari (1997)), and the English name of the feature. We also note where the place name is mentioned in the text and refer to pictures in the book.

Several places mentioned in the stories are not within the scope of the map. We chose to show only a small portion of the Tetlin area in order to give sufficient detail.

For those who wish to locate the area on a map of Alaska, the closest town is Tok (about 25 miles northwest of Tetlin). Since Tok, however, is not a traditional (or even very old) settlement, we chose not to include it on the map.

Map num.	**Upper Tanana name**	**Literal translation**	**English name**
1	Nahk’ade	‘fishing place’	Last Tetlin
	• *Mentioned in Chapters 1, 3, 5, and 9; picture on p. 31*		
2	Łuugn Mann’	‘fish lake’	group of lakes near Last Tetlin village
	• *Mentioned in Chapter 1; picture on p. 9*		
3	Talttheedn (Mann’)	‘water drops (lake)’	Taltheadamund Lake
	• *Mentioned in Chapters 1 and 5*		
4	Nudh’ąą Mann’	‘island lake’	Nuziamund Lake
	• *Mentioned in Chapter 1*		

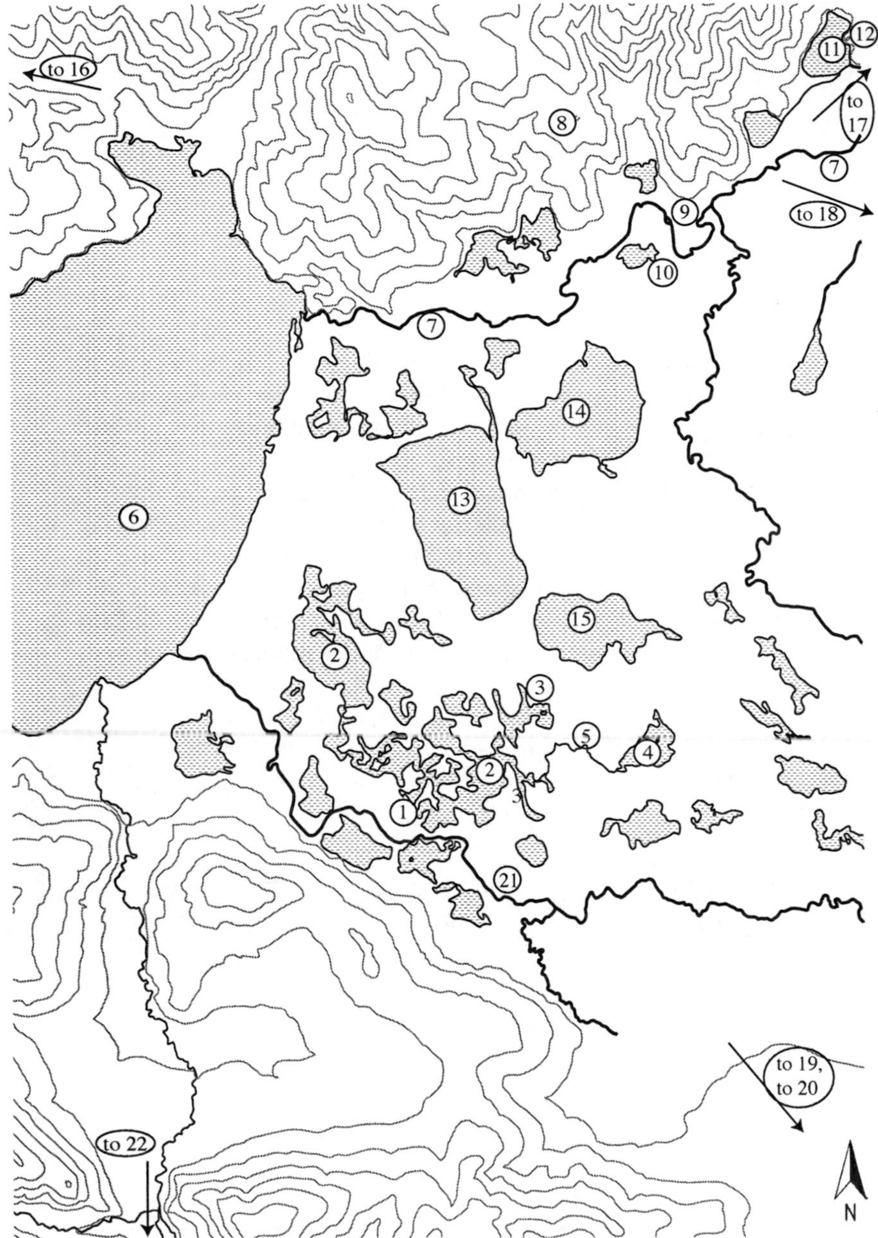

Tetlin area, with locations mentioned in Cora David's stories.

Map num.	Upper Tanana name	Literal translation	English name
5	K’ąy Ch’it Niign	‘twisted willow creek’	creek leading out of Nuziamund Lake
	• *Mentioned in Chapter 1*		
6	Manh Choh	‘big lake’	Tetlin Lake
	• *Mentioned in Chapters 5, 8, and 9; picture on p. 30*		
7	Teedląy Niign	‘current flows river’	Tetlin River
	• *Mentioned in 13; picture on p. 30*		
8	Teedląy Ddhal’	‘current flows mountain’	Tetlin Hill
	• *Mentioned in Chapters 11, 12; picture on p. 74*		
9	Teedląy Keey	‘current flows village’	Tetlin Village
	• *Mentioned in Chapter 12; picture on p. 75*		
10	Tl’oh Oogn Mann’	‘lake among the grass’	Skate Lake
	• *Picture on p. 75*		
11	Ts’iit Tl’oo Mann’	‘porcupine grass lake’	Porcupine Grass L.
	• *Mentioned in Chapter 10; picture on p. 63*		
12	Ts’iit Tl’oo Ddhal’	‘porcupine grass mountain’	?
	• *Picture on p. 63*		
13	Daałal Mann’	‘butterfly lake’	Dathlamund Lake
	• *Picture on p. 75*		
14	Goo Choh Mann’	‘big ? lake’[1]	Gasoline Lake
	• *Picture on p. 75*		
15	Tinii’ah Mann’	‘points in a direction lake’	Old Albert Lake
	• *Mentioned in Chapter 9; picture on p. 75*		
16	Dihthaad	‘nearby place’	Tanacross
	• *Mentioned in Chapter 10*		
17	Toochin’ Mann’	‘sticks in water lake’	Midway Lake
	• *Mentioned in Chapter 10; picture on p. 37*		
18	Naambia	‘ripples on water’[2]	Northway
	• *Mentioned in Chapter 3*		
19	Uudladn	‘the one that is melting’	
	• *Mentioned in Chapter 3*		
20	K’įį Shyüh Niign	‘birch ridge creek’	mountain at Kinshuda
	• *Mentioned in Chapter 3*		

Map num.	Upper Tanana name	Literal translation	English name
21	Sh'aat Niign	'my wife creek'[3]	Wife Creek
	• *Mentioned in Chapter 3*		
22	Chehtsadn Niign	'mice creek'	Mice Creek
	• *Mentioned in Chapter 3*		

Notes

1. Kari (1997, item 74) notes this lake as Gǫǫ Choh Manh 'big rhubarb lake'. Cora does not accept the pronunciation with the nasal vowel, nor the suggested translation.
2. Kari (1997, item 230) tentatively glosses Naambia Niign, the Nabesna river, as 'stone creek'. The translation here follows Roy Sam of Northway.
3. Kari (1997, item 146) also lists the forms Sh'aa Niign and Sh'ąą Niign.

Teedląy t'iin naholndak niign

Stories by the Tetlin People

Part I

Nidhihshyąą niign

Part I

Stories of how I grew up

1

Nee’eł stsakijeexal xa nahogndak

Niithaad *I think it’s in 1970s somewhere*
Neg Nahk’ade nts’ą’
neekeey nts’ą’ natsetnaa.
Negn Nahk’adn <<dą’>>
haatage dą’ niits’indeel eł.
Gary ntsuul <eł>
Danny chih ntsuul nts’ą’
Roy eł shin eł shįį <<t’eey>> hu’eł ts’ą’natsetdak.

Anaann’ łaatag tüh naann’ skets’etdeel eł <ts’ayh> guuy <<łaakey>>
shin shiign eetąą,
ts’ayh guuy,
detl’oon eł eltsiin,
łaakey ishyiit eetąą.

Gary, “Jan shyiit t’eey naann’ skets’uudeeł,” shehnih.
“Ts’ayh ntsuul nts’ą’ ch’a tsaadiil?” udihnih.

❧ 1 ❧

I talk about how the boat capsized with us

In this narrative, Cora talks about several boating accidents that happened when she was traveling in the Last Tetlin area with several family members.

A long time ago, I think in the 1970s
Up at 'fish trap' (Last Tetlin)[1]
we moved back to our camp.
Up there at Last Tetlin
we tried to cross the river.
Gary was small and
And Danny was also small.
Just Roy and I were walking around with them.

We came to the crossing and there were two little boats lying there,

little canoes,
made with canvas,
two of them were lying there.

"This is how we're going to go across," Gary said to me.
"The canoe is small, how could we go across in it?" I said to him.

Ay t’oot’eey chih
“Ushyiit įįhaayh,” <shehnih>.
Ushyiit ihshyah tl’aan
shiign dhihdah.
Noo’ dii du’ tach’et’oh dą’ eedah.

Noo’ ch’ats’inįįkįį eł
ts’ayh gaay tinįįłaat nee’eł neeshiign tah neetlade k’eh tuu nel’ąą
 t’oot’eey Gary Gary du’ tach’et’oh ay t’oot’eey
tinįįłaat t’oot’eey.

Ay eł
Danny eł dita’ eł hitloo:: nah’aanug,
tl’oh shyiit t’eey nahtetduuk nts’ą’ hidloh.
Gary chih edloh <eł>
k’a’ udhihnih nts’ą’ “Nuhtahjakk’aa!” hudihnih.
Ay eł k’a hedloh k’e dahǫdątsat nts’ą’
nih shii chihdelshyah nts’ą’ shihnih’įh.

Eł
Danny ntsuul t’oot’eey
“Ts’ayh gaay iin naann’ łits’inuhtl’uh tl’aan ay shyiit,”
tach’et’oo eł
“shnaa <hanuhts’ąyh> shyiit ditaadaał
“anuhts’ąy’ ay shyiit ditaahaał Gary naann’ sketsaakeeł.”
Noo’ detshyag eł skets’inįįkįįh.
Hǫǫsu’ t’eey k’etl’ahts’eedeeł, naann’.
Roy eł Danny eł kah chih natetkįį nts’ą’ noo’ skehuuneedlah.

Jan ch’a tsąą ts’ą’ t’eey hutshyaak t’oot’eey k’a hǫǫt’eey ts’eniign.
Hu’atsaan t’eey k’a hulshyaak.

Hahnde’ <<K’ąy’ Ch’it Niign ts’eedeeł Nudh’ąą Mann’ hahnde’>>
 Taltheedn ts’an <<Łuugn Mann’>> chih idzideeł tl’aan hahnde’.

But
"You go in it," he told me.
I went inside and
I sat at the back.
He sat in the front where he could paddle.

We start out and
that little boat went under the water and the water came up to our waists
and Gary, Gary was still paddling, even though
even though the boat was under water.

And
Danny and his father were laughing up on the land,
they were crawling around in the grass and they were laughing.
Gary also was laughing and
I picked up a gun and "I'll shoot you guys!" I said to them.
And then they stopped laughing and
they held their laugh back and they looked at me.

And
Danny was small but:
"Let's tie the little canoes together and in it"
and he paddled
"my mother will sit on one side,
Gary will sit on the other side and we will paddle across."
He did what Danny told him and so we paddled across.
We made it across nicely.
He canoed back over to Roy and Danny and took them over to the other side.
A funny thing happened there, but we never told anyone.
A very funny thing happened for them.

There at 'twisted willow creek' we were going; we went from 'island lake' to 'water drops lake' and then we walked over that and we

chitseedeeł.
Haniign nįįłąy
ay
nahugn ts'ayh choh nahtet-hiik, noodlee ts'ayy'.
Choh.
Hunaann' Nudh'ąą nįįłąy tüh naann' sketseedeel ha hunaann'
skehiine'ah <ts'ehłag ts'ayh> du'
<sts'iiniin'> Danny yuuton'.
Nuhts'ayy' <chih> dineh yuuton',
naann' tsiił k'eh uk'e sketsedeel ha.

Naann' ihhaal eł naann' ihhaal eł t'eey
ts'ayh tthitohnia eł ninihshyay eł t'eey
sts'iiniin'
ts'ayh dehxįą eł t'eey eł sts'aa tehdeexał nts'ą'
tinagntth'at ay t'oot'eey
k'a jil t'eey łanihthat t'oot'eey
k'at'eey nts'ą' deedihnay nts'ą' k'etladhihshyah.
Shik'eegn t'oot'eey.
Hǫǫ i'eł tah ch'a ts'iikeey gaay iin dąy,
natseetndeek niign t'eey *anyway* t'eey neeheh'įh.

Hǫǫ shįį' dihniił.

put our boat in 'fish lake'.
The creek was flowing
and
they carried around a big boat, an aluminum boat.[2]
A big one.
We were trying to cross the creek coming out of 'island lake' and when we were crossing, on one side
my son Danny was holding on.
He was holding on to one side of the canoe,
we crossed on it like on a bridge.

I was walking across and
I was in the center of the boat
my son
rocked the boat and then the boat capsized and
I fell in and
almost drowned but
I never said anything, I just walked up.
I was really mad though.
It's always like that with young people,
wherever we move, they do that.

That's about all I say.

Notes

1. Cora also mentions the old name *Naadeel* for Last Tetlin. Cora's camp in the area was called *Tsiił Choh* 'big bridge'.
2. *Literally:* a white man's boat.

Ann Adam, mother of Cora's father (child's identity not known).

Łuugn Mann' (2), a group of lakes near Last Tetlin. (Numbers in captions are cross-referenced to the map and table of place names on pages xix–xxii.) © Jessica Cherry and Forest Kirst, December 2010.

2

Neetsay choh shitthiishnihshyay xa nahogndak

Neekeey, neeshyah gaay nts'ą'
1956 I think
I have to say that in English that because
nobody knows how to say this in our language
but 1956 we noo' nats'andał neeshyah gaay nts'ą'
shta' shnaa eł
sts'iiniin' Danny eł
shin eł.
Hǫǫ dan ts'elt'eh.
Chinh maagn noo'
nats'atdal eł t'eey shta' iin ttheh na'ihdaał.

Eł t'eey
neetsay ch'uutnexon dihtth'ąą łii iin <łahtthagn nts'ą'>
shtl'ade aan dą hiidhakchüh,
huutl'uul' eł
łii iin huut'ah shihdįnay eł daahuunih'at.

2

I talk about how a big bear really scared me

Cora has told me this story many times to warn me of bears. Note that several times throughout the story (and also in other stories), she uses the English word bear *or the Upper Tanana word* neetsay *'our grandfather' when referring to the bear. The word* shoh *'black bear' is* įįjii *(taboo), and Cora does not like to use it.*

Our camp, our little cabin
1956 I think
I have to say that in English that because
nobody knows how to say this in our language
we were coming back from our little cabin and
with my father and my mother and
my child Danny and
myself.
We were four people.
At the edge of the flats
we were going back and I was walking way ahead of my parents.

And
I heard a bear growling and all the dogs
I had tied them up around my waist,
with their rope
the dogs threw me down, so I turned them loose.

Shk’eh taanih hu’udihnay
ts’ał shyiit tah
stach’idzihneetl’a nts’ą’ hukol.
Shin shįį t’eey <neetsay> nts’ą’ na’ihthat,
k’a’ gaay eł.

Shta’ iin niitah shta’ iin shnaa eł nahitdee.
“Shoh!”
shta’ idihnih.
“Shiign ut’aat t’eey tidhinlt’ayh,” shehnih.
Nagnjii:t k’at’eey ut’aat i’ogt’ay nihthan.
Neetsay du’ *anyway* neetsay du’ huu
ch’uutnexon nts’ą’ esał.
Shta’: “Shii::gn!” shehnay eł shiign ut’aat t’a’ t’idhagnt’ay eł shta’ niints’ą’ t’eey yuunihdak <eł>.
Iigaan t’aat naann’ t’eey dehk’aa ha,
neetsay <<t’atnelnay nts’ą’ almoh>>.
Huu’altthat nts’ą’ huu’altthat nts’ą’ t’eey nahne’ tanatidhagtthat nts’ą’ niitah shnaa naht’aag tana’ihtthat.

Ishyiit dą’
k’at’eey k’at’eey ihshyaan nts’ą’ ts’iniin ihłiin eł.
Sht’ayy’ hǫǫłįį
t’oot’eey
dishnii:: nts’ą’ shxu’ <chih> t’eey diishnaa.
Tuu nihthiid tl’aan hantee::y t’eey tuu nelkon’ shtl’adiintsat eł
“Innah!
“<Łahtthagn nts’ą’> dendiihi k’at’eey hǫǫ tįįdiil innah de’,” shehnay eł hǫdihshah.

Ishyiit ch’a neetsay shitthiishnihshyah.
Ay t’oot’eey ishyiit ts’an noo’ t’eey k’a ukah nagnjidn hǫǫ t’eey ay nah’ogn ts’ał shyiit natihdii.

I thought they were going to protect me, [instead]
into the brush
they ran away and were gone.[1]
I stood up to the bear alone
with a small gun.

My father and my mother were standing way back there.
"A bear!"
I said to my father.
"Lay down on the ground below [in front of] him," he said to me.
I was scared, I didn't want to lie below him.
As for the bear,
it was growling and roared.
My father: "Down!" he said to me and I lay down below him and my father shot him from way back there.
He shot him right under the arm
the bear << tumbled and rolled over>>.
I ran away, I ran away, I ran way back and I stood behind my mother.

At that time
I wasn't fully grown, I was just a kid.
I was strong
but
I was shaking and my teeth were chattering.
My mother heated up water and quickly she gave me hot water and
"Drink it!
"You'll stop shaking if you drink this," she said to me and I did it.

That's when the bear really scared me.
Even after that I was not afraid to go out in the woods.

Transcribed and translated with the help of Avis and Roy Sam.

Notes

1. Cora says she never saw them again.

3

Sh’aat Niign[1] negn natsetneegn xa nahogndak

Ihtsuul dą’[2] shta’ iin eł
Nahk’ade ts’an huna’ degn
K’įį Shyüh Niign
naann’ Sh’aat Niign nts’ą’
natsetndeek.
Diniign kah <nts’ą> ni’eełhełe’.
Tsuugn eł
tthiikaan
<nts’ą’>
huugn ha ni’eełhełe’ ha huhnatsetdak.

Shta’, “Hanaat, Uudlade dą’ nts’ą’
shk’e tl’üdn noo’ de’ t’eey ishyiit sǫ’ ni’ųshyah,” shehnih <eł>.
“Dii xa’ hudihnay eł neetsay, shoh choh ishyiit nii’edah,” shehnih.

I’agndayh.

3

I talk about moving about in the area of 'my wife creek'

This narrative illustrates how Cora grew up moving around, mainly between Nahk'ade ('fish trap') and Sh'aat Niign ('my wife creek').

When I was little, my parents
from 'fish trap' (Last Tetlin) up that way
[is] 'birch ridge creek'
up to 'my wife creek'
we moved there.
For moose, and they're setting traps.
Marten and
wolf
and
they're setting traps for all of those, that's why we're walking there.

My father, "To 'the one with moss'
don't go there even long after I'm gone," he said to me.
"Because I tell you that 'our grandfathers', big bears, hibernate[3] there,"
he said to me.
I remember.

Niithoo t'eey Sh'aat Niign dą' dzaltth'i'.
Ch'a ts'aa'utneet'eh t'oot'eey.

Ay tl'aan eł
Chehtsade Niign degn ch'itseeynaa.
Ishyiit shii
Chehtsade Niign
tthil eł
diniign eł kah natetneegn ahuh natetdak
hu'eł tidhihshah.
Chinh tüh naann'
saan xa taht'eey ts'edak t'oot'eey k'at'eey
k'at'eey niihetdagn nts'ą' hǫǫ t'eey ishyiit ndee ntsą' hiihteedeeł dą' ts'ą' hihteedak, i'agndayh.

Hǫǫ shįį'.

We stayed at 'my wife creek' for a long time.
I didn't like it though.

And then
we moved up to 'mice creek'.
There
'mice creek'
mountain squirrels and
and moose, they move there for them, they move around there
I went with them.
Over the flats
we barely made it [with exhaustion] but still
they didn't stay there, they just went on to the place where they were going and there they stopped, I remember that.

That's it.

Transcribed and translated with the help of Avis and Roy Sam.

Notes

1. Cora frequently pronounces 'sh'aat' as 'sh'aa'.
2. Cora was about 14 at the time.
3. The Upper Tanana verb form means 'they stay there'; Avis Sam suggests that Cora is talking about hibernation.

4

Nan' na'etnaa xa nahogndak

1944 <dą'>
ts'iikeey guuy ts'įįłįį eł
9 years old, 8 years old.
Nan' naa'etnah
ch'ittheh.

K'ahdu' k'a hǫǫ hohdiign
k'at'eey hits'etnay.
Nan' naa'etnaa.
"Ehts'ayh cho::h!"
ts'iiniithan.
Natsetdak <<nts'ą'>> nats'etdeeyh tah
<nan'> nahshiign nan' neet'aat ske'eljii.
Ay
k'a hits'itnay dii ch'a dąy' ts'uunih.

Ishyiit dą' hǫǫ hutshyaak dą' t'eey chih
saa chih

4

I talk about the [1944] earthquake

This narrative begins as a story about the 1944 earthquake and morphs into a reflection on language use and former language policy.

In 1944
we were little children and
9 years old, 8 years old.
The earth moved
for the first time.

Now it's not like it used to be
we did not know.
The earth was shaking.
"It's really windy!"
we were thinking.
When we walked, when we stood up,
the ground was sliding back and forth underneath us.
And
we didn't know, we never thought what it was.

At the time this happened
the sun, too

t'a'įį'ąh
nah'ogn
utnatl'aa::t eł dziin t'eey.
<<Ishyiit dą' chih san t'eey natetdeeyh t'oot'eey k'a hǫǫdihnay.
Detl'oon eł ts'enehtl'uh tl'aan xee shyiit tats'ehłeeg tl'aan tuutiił tth'aak shyiit ts'enihts'ah.>>

Ts'inelji::t.
"Nts'ą' hutshyaak?" ts'ineethan.
K'at'eey hǫǫ hiits'etnay eł
ts'įįtsuul nts'ą'
neenaa iin t'eey
k'a hiihitnay
ishyiit hǫǫ hutshyaak dą'.

Shta' shįį'
huugn
<<dinahtl'aa >> [ch']uusii eł
hii'etnayh eł.
"Nan' naa'etnaa dįį," nee'ehnih.
Dii da'ehnay ts'uudnih,
ishyiit hųųdą' k'at'eey,
k'at'eey noodlee k'eh <<tthahdzilxoo'>>.
Neek'eh shįį' ts'ehǫǫheey.

Ishyiit
<xach'uuneltan shyah> dą' dats'iniideel eł ishyiit dą' ch'a
"K'at'eey nuhk'eh hutahheel," neehinih.
Dii nts'ą' hach'aneehenay <<eł>>
daats'indeel nts'ą' shta' hǫǫ its'inay eł shta'.
"<Ishyiit dą'> nuhts'ą' huhheey tah
"noodlee k'eh
"nuhts'ą' huhheek
"k'a shtahtthagn'," nee'ehnih.

it went under
out there
it became dark, even though it was day.
At that time, the stars were falling, but I never said anything.
We braided canvas and we put grease in and we lit it in a saucer.

We were scared.
"What's happening?" we thought.
We didn't know and
we were little
even our mothers
didn't know
what was happening there.

Only my father
things
he read in books
he knew.
"There is an earthquake," he said to us
We didn't know what he was talking about,
at that time,
we did not speak English.
We only spoke our language.

At that time
we attended school and there
"You're not going to speak in your language," they told us.
We were wondering why and
we went to my father and we told him about it.
"These times when I spoke to you girls
"in English
"I spoke to you girls
"you never listened to me," he told us.

"Hǫǫ ch'ale'
"tthahtdalxoo' xa ch'ale'
"ishyiit ts'an noo' hǫǫ.
"Dahniil ha ch'ale nuhts'ą' noodlee k'eh huhheey," nee'ehnih.

K'at'eey shta' dziitth'agn hoonih t'oot'eey
xach'uuneltan dą' nats'eniideel eł
neehehtsüh
neek'eh ts'ehǫǫheey tah.
Ay
"Dii xa ch'a neeheh'ąy?" ts'iinehtthiig.

Hahnoo' eł
t'axoh hiits'etnay eł
hǫǫtl'aan neeheh'ąy ts'iiniithan.
Hǫǫ shįį'.

"That's the way
"you're supposed to be speaking
"from that time on.
"That's why I speak to you girls in English," he said to us.

We didn't listen to my father, but
we went to school and
they spanked us
when we spoke in our language.
And
"Why are they doing this to us?" we would think.

Much later
we found out why
we finally found out why they did that.
That's all.

Transcribed and translated with the help of Cora David.

5

Ihtsuul dą’ nts’ą’ ts’eneeshyaan xa nahogndak

Ts’įįtsuul dą’ Nahk’ade dą’ ch’ale ts’eneeshyaan,
shaadeh iin shoondaa iin shchil iin shdia’ iin eł shnaa shta’ <<eł>>.

Aadaat du’ Tommy Paul
diits’iikeey iin <<dii’aat eł>> hihdeltth’ih ay iin du’.

Ts’eeneek tah neekeey
nunįįk’ul dą’ t’eey neekeey,
Taltthεedn noo’ dą’ nits’eneek.
Dzanh xa ni’eełhełeegn ha shnaa iin.
Neexon du’ ts’įįtsuul nts’ą’ k’at’eey dzanh xa t’eey ni’eełts’edleegn nts’ą’.
Ts’iikeey ts’įįłįį nts’ą’
dzelxoo.
Neenaa iin ts’eneh’ąy k’eh ts’etdiik taamaagn łoots’itdak nts’ą’

k’a łą eeł <<nits’etleek>> t’oot’eey,

~ 5 ~

I talk about being young and growing up

This is the first of a set of short narratives where Cora talks about growing up "the old way." This story describes the annual migration and subsistence cycle.

When we were little, we grew up in Last Tetlin,
with my older sisters, my older brothers, my younger brothers, my
younger sisters and my parents.
Down there Tommy Paul
and his wife and children lived.

We moved our campsite;
it was a little ways to our camp,
we moved to 'water drops' [lake].
My parents set traps for muskrat.
Us, we were too small, we didn't set traps for muskrat.

We were kids,
just playing.
We watched our parents and we copied them and we walked around the
lakeshore
we didn't really set traps,

dzelxoh nts'ą' ni'eełts'ełeek ts'ihol'iik.
Dzanh xa.
Shnaa iin shta' iin
ntl'aa::n <<dzanh>> t'eey nahelshyeek.

K'at'eey nat'uts'ełeegn k'a hiits'etnay nts'ą'
"Nat'u'ahłe'," neehindii nts'ą'.
K'a hiits'itnay nts'ą' k'a-t'eey hǫǫ ts'etdiign.

Ay tl'aan
dzanh iin huts'ehk'aayh tl'aan huts'ehgąy tl'aan dogn daats'ełeeg tl'aan.
Shnaa ch'ale hǫǫdiidį' <<tsat>> dit'aat dehjiit nts'ą'.

Dzanh eegąyh, ntl'aa::n t'eey.
Ishyiit daahilshyeek.
Nats'e'iił, dzanh eegąy nats'e'iił dą' nsǫǫ!

Ay tl'aan tah,
"T'axoh, natsutnaa'!" hendii nts'ą'.
Negn Nahk'ade nts'ą' tanatsetdak k'a jah <Teedląy'> nts'ą' k'a natsetdiik nts'ą' Nahk'ade.
Nahk'ade shyiit nts'ą' natsetdiih.
Łuugn delgayh ay xa shihdeltth'iik łuugn hek'aay.
<<Łuugn>> hiiyehk'aay tl'aan <<dahdzał shyiit hahdogn >> daahiiyelshyeek nts'ą'.
Ntl'aa:n t'eey huundayh,
xay nihthaad hendii nts'ą'.
<Xay xah niihoholshyeek.>

Hǫǫ ch'ale <<hetdiign>> k'ahdu' dziin
k'a hiidlaan nah'ogn ntsiin iin hǫǫhetdiik.
Shiin tah Nahk'ade nts'ą' hihtetdak nts'ą' łuugn hehk'aay xa hihtendeek ahneg.
K'ahdu' t'eey hǫǫhetdį'.

we played, we pretended to set traps.
For muskrat.
My parents
brought back lots of muskrat.

We didn't help to skin them, we didn't know how and,
"You skin it out," they used to tell us.
We didn't know how to do it, so we didn't do it.

And then
We fileted the muskrat and they we dried them, we put them up [on a drying rack].
My mother was the one that used to do it; she put wood under it [to make smoke].
The muskrats dried, lots of them.
They put them up there.
When we ate dry muskrat, it was so good!

And then,
"Enough, let's move on!" they said.
We moved back to Last Tetlin, we didn't move back to 'current flows' (Tetlin), but to Last Tetlin.
Last Tetlin, that's where we went.
A whole bunch of them stayed there for whitefish, so they can cut fish.
They fileted the fish and put it on the fish rack.

They got lots,
there's a long winter ahead, they say.
They prepare for winter.

That's what they do today,
not very many, but some still do that.
In summer they all go to Last Tetlin; they move up there to cut fish.

They do that even today.

Neg Manh Choh maagn ishyiit nts’ą’ chih hihtetdak dineh iin nahelseey diniign kah ay chih hehk’aay tl’aan hiiyehgąy’.
Hiithüh <chih>,
ts’exeh iin hiixa etndah nts’ą’ <<hiixa’ ha’et’üh tl’aan ushyiit shi’ ts’ąy natthał eł hahiiyehłeeg ay tl’aan uuxa’ ts’ąy seey eł hahiiyehcheey’ ch’iijeey k’it>>.
Hiiyehthoh tl’aan <<etthey eł>> kantsįą eł jiyh eł
diinadzelshyay hii’eł exąą.

Shnaa udzih eek xay tah nadzulshyaagn ay t’eey exąą,
naatl’ade eł yimaagn hohtsiik.
Nadzeelshyaak xay tah.
Ushyiit dziinaats’eljiiyh <chih>
chih mboh iin k’eh chih mboh
dziinaaheljiiy ay k’eh ts’etdiik nts’ą’.
<Łahtth’agn nts’ą’> uxa’ hadetdah.
Shnaa neents’ą’ ts’anii’elt’eek.
<Hǫǫchaa t’eey yaa etndaa’ k’at’eey hǫǫsu’ nts’ą’ uk’ats’enehta’.>
Ay eł dziinaats’eljiiyh.
Udzih eek.

Hǫǫ ch’ale ts’eneeshyaan.

Men also went up there to the shore of Tetlin Lake to hunt for moose;
    they also fileted and dried it.
Their skins too,
women work on it and cut the hair off and they take the inside layer
    off with a flesher, and then they scrape it with a knife over a little
    wooden scraping board.
They scrape it and when it's really soft, moccasins, mittens,
whatever they wear, they make out of it.

My mother used to make winter parkas out of caribou skins,
she used to fix beads all around them.
Parkas for winter.
We slide downhill on our stomachs in it too,
just like in a toboggan; with a toboggan
they slide, and we copy them.
All the hair came off.
My mother gets mad at us.
She worked so hard for it and we didn't take care of it.
We slid down on our stomachs.
Caribou parkas.

That's how we grew up.

Transcribed and translated with the help of Cora David.

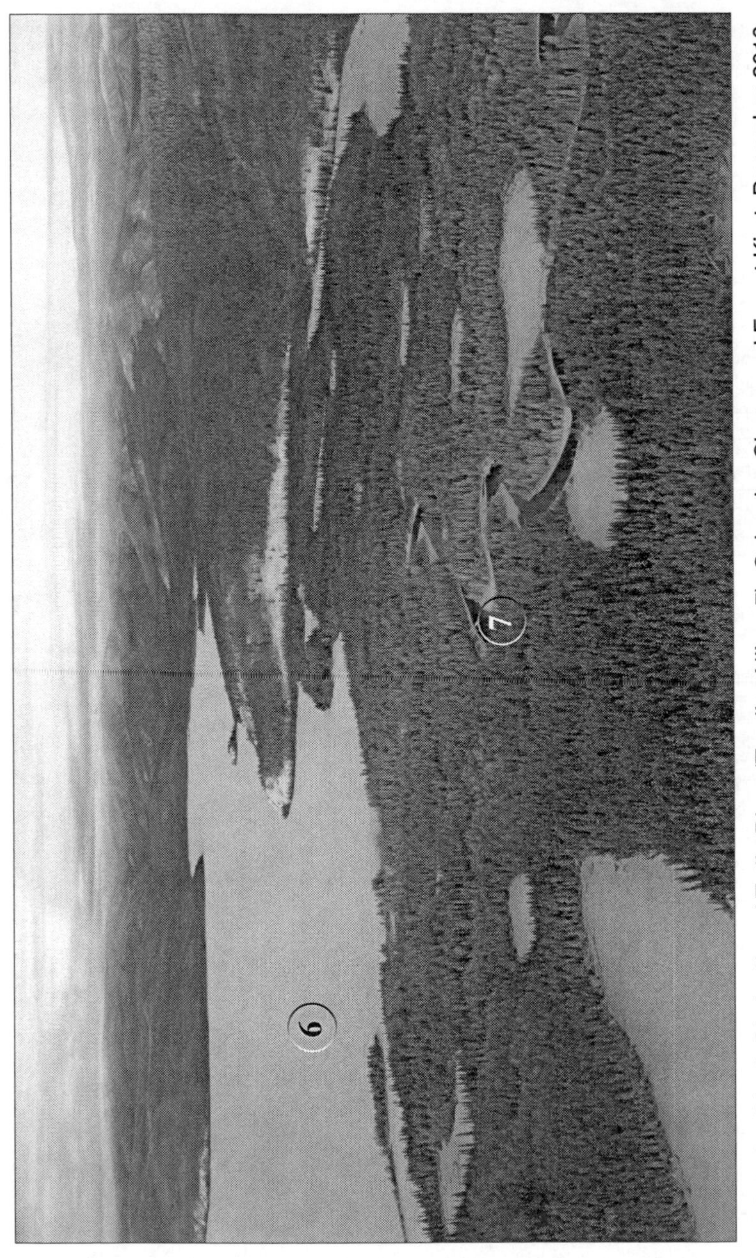

Tetlin Lake (Manh Choh, 6) and Tetlin River (Teedlay Niign, 7). © Jessica Cherry and Forest Kirst, December 2010.

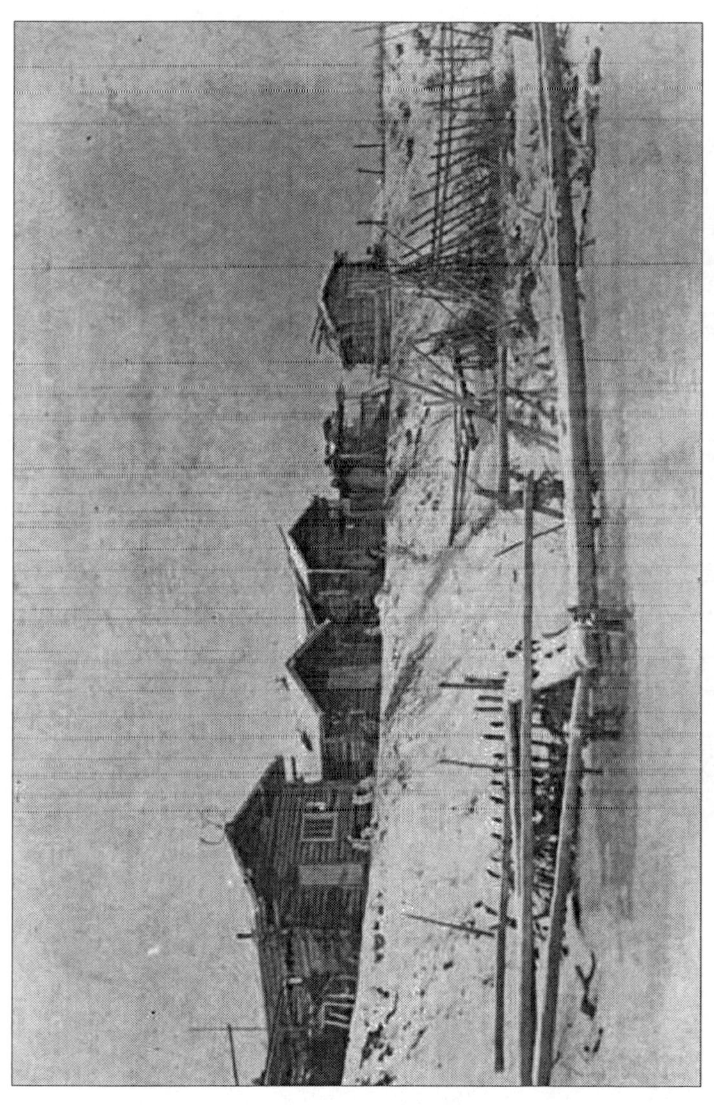

Last Tetlin (Nahk'ade, 1) showing fish traps. Frederick B. Drane Collection, UAF-1991-46-674. Alaska and Polar Regions Collections, Elmer E. Rasmuson Library, University of Alaska Fairbanks.

6

Shi' ts'e'aal xa nahogndak

Shi' t'eey nits'ehchik ha'
gah tat'eey nits'ehchik
gah tat'eey nits'ehchik nts'ą' dits'an t'eey
nits'ehchik ts'ehk'aayh.
<Ishyiit dą' k'at'eey shi' ushyiit neltan huułay ch'ikol.>
<Łahtthag nts'ą' t'eey shi' ts'ehgąy tl'aan ch'inshyiit shyiit nats'elshyeek.>
Ts'ehk'aayh nts'ą' ts'ehgąy tl'aan taats'elshyeek.

Ntl'aa::n t'eey ts'uunday tl'aan eł
ch'itdanh nts'ą' ch'its'endeek.
Udzih, udzih iin neeshyah de' <chih> udzih kah ts'aadał ishyiit de' <chih> ts'ahk'aayh tl'aan stsaats'alshyeek udzih.
Huuthüh du' tahiidethoh nts'ą'
eek hii'eł exaan
huugn.
Hishyiit dal'iad kee huugn t'eey hii'eł exąą.
Neeta' iin du' hugn niiduuy eł huugn

6

I talk about the food we eat

This narrative discusses the kinds of food Cora and her family used to eat. Poor nutrition is a problem in many Northern communities, and Cora is very concerned about this. The benefits of eating traditional foods are one of her favorite topics.

We used to put up even meat,
we used to put up rabbit
we used to put up rabbit and ducks even,
we put it up and we fileted it.
At that time, there was no freezer.
We dried all the meat and we put it in the cache.

We fileted it and we dried it and then we put it away.

We take lots and then
we move to a different place.
A whole band of caribou came in; when we went for caribou, we also fileted it and put it away, the caribou.
They scrape the skins and
make clothes out of them
and things.
They even fix their footwear with it.
Our fathers, lynx and things

nǫǫgaay
tsuugn eł huugn tah ha'eełhedlak nts'ą'.
Ntl'aa:n t'eey nahelshyiik.
Tthiikaan tat'eey
an nahiitelshyeegn ha.
Ay tl'aan hiithüh eł jiyh ch'i'exaan tl'aan
kantsįą t'eey hii'eł exąą.
Tthiishyooh,
tsa' tthiishyooh *they call it those* <hii'eł exąą>.

Hǫǫ ch'ale ts'ineeshyaan.
Shk'eh <łahtthagn nts'ą'> huhheyh de',
ihtsuul dą' ts'an nats'otelnak de',
ishyiit huunoo' ch'a łą',
hǫǫsǫǫ nts'ą' t'eey ts'eneeshyah.
K'ahdu' du'
hugn
ch'utkeedn shyah dats'etdak nts'ą' hugn shi' tah ts'uukeet nts'ą' diithuugn.
<K'atmbah k'e eltsiin[1]> tat'eey ts'uutkeet nts'ą'
nuhxa hǫǫsǫǫ nts'ą' hǫǫsu' nts'ą' t'eey
<k'a t'eey staniinatdeey nts'ą' nuhxa hǫǫsǫǫ' maatahtnda'>
hǫǫchaa t'eey mbaatadenda tl'aan ha ch'ale.
Shi' nts'ą' t'eey ch'a hǫǫsu' nts'ą' ts'e'aał.

fox
marten and other things, they trap for them.
They bring back lots.
Even wolf
they sell them.
And they make mittens with the skins and
slippers they make with them.
Hats,
what they call beaver hats, they make with them.

That's how we were brought up.
If I speak only in my language,
if we tell stories about when I was young,
from that far-back time of my life,
we grew up really well.
But nowadays
things
we go to the store in order to buy meat and things there.

We buy chicken and
it's easy for you, it is good
you don't worry and it works fine for you, you have to work for it,
you have to work hard for it.
We eat all kinds of food, it's good.

Transcribed and translated with the help of Cora David.

Notes

1. A coinage by Cora: 'the thing that looks like willow grouse' = chicken

Four Adam children (from left): Ellia, Franklin, Linberg, Cora. Tetlin Photograph Collection, UAF-1987-0224-54, Alaska and Polar Regions Collections, Elmer E. Rasmuson Library, University of Alaska Fairbanks.

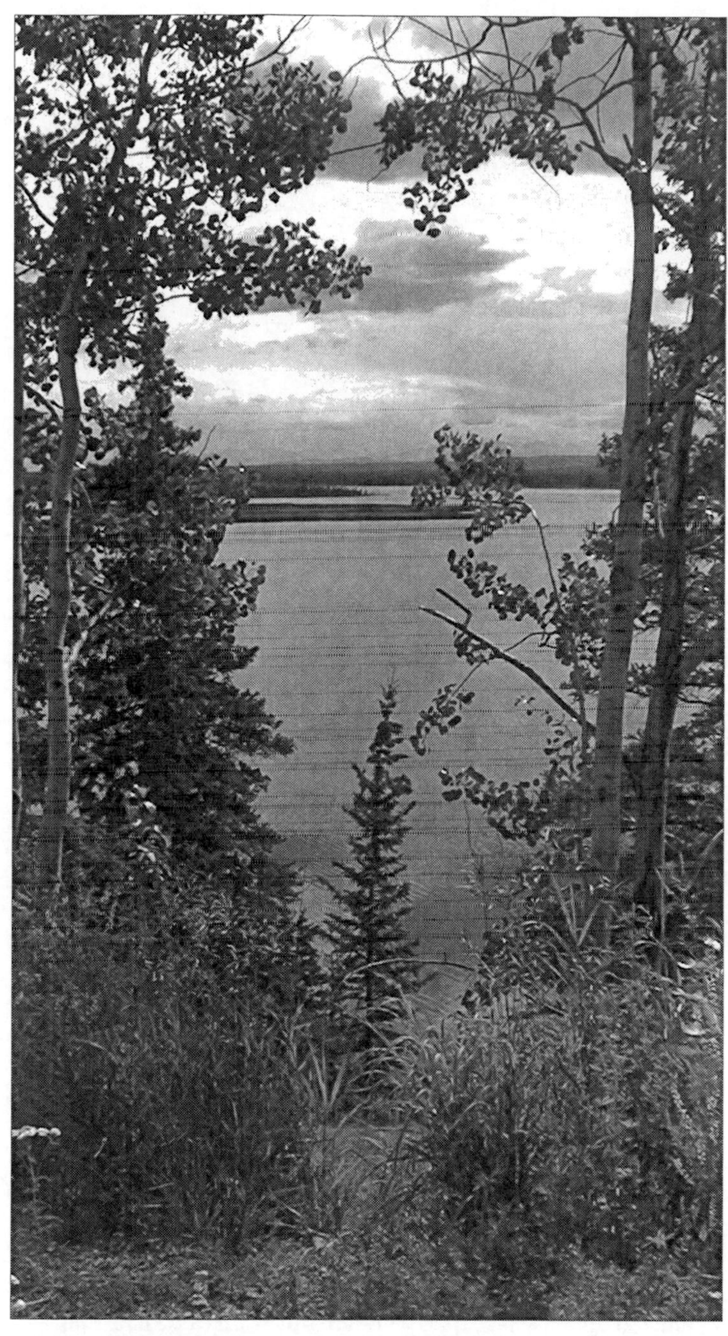

Midway Lake (Toochin' Mann', 17). © Olga Lovick, June 2010.

7

Mel dzelxoo xa nahogndak

Ts'įįtsuul dą'
Dziin Choh Dziin'
hǫǫłįį tah shnaa
neexa
ts'iiniin shyiign
nayneekįį nts'ą'.
Ts'iikeey shyiign gaay exaan ay neetlah ełeeg.
Ay t'eey neexa nsǫǫ.

Shta' chih
k'įį eł t'eey hu mboh ehtsiik shchil iin xa.
Dichinh, dichinh
huugn
dichinh ełįį maagn hohtsiik tl'aan
hiiyuutǫǫ mbįįt'ah chiit hiiyuutǫǫ da chih hohtsiik eł.
Ay tl'aan gah ke' k'e et'ii'aay łii huuxa ehtsiik.
Ay eł t'eey hihdelxoo, huuxa hǫǫsǫǫ.

K'ahdu' dziin du' dii ts'iikeey iin huh diitl'aa:n t'eey neexa ukeedn heniik nts'ą'

7

I talk about toys

A discussion of the toys Cora's parents made for her and her siblings.

When we were little
Christmas Day
when it was, my mother
for us
dolls
she sewed them.
She made little dolls and gave them to us.
And we really liked them.

My father too
made toboggans out of birch wood for my younger brothers.
Wood, wood
things
he made a wooden frame on top of it and
he also made handles behind the toboggan.
And then he would cut rabbits' feet and made them look like dogs.
And they played with it lots, they really liked it.

Today's kids ask us for expensive stuff and

huuxa ts'iiyuukiit.
Neexon du' dą' ch'a ts'eneeshyaan,
k'at'eey huuk'e ts'iniishyeel.
Huugn
dzilxoo tah jih dah'ogn neenaa iin tsahetdiik niign <<k'eh>> t'eey dzilxoo jį'.

Łuugn xa dahdzał guuy <chih> ts'ehtsiik dze huugn ch'it'aan iin łuugn ts'il'iik nts'ą'
dahdzał k'it dahuuts'itleeg nts'ą' huuts'ehk'ay' ts'ehol'iik nts'ą'.
Dziin uudih t'eey huhdzelxuu kon'tsiil ts'ehol'iik.

Hǫǫ ch'ale ts'eneeshyąą neexon du' k'at'eey hǫǫsu' nts'ą' aats'ineeshyeel t'oot'eey neexa hǫǫsǫǫ::: nts'ą'.
Huu'inih dii eł t'eey dzelxoh.
Neenaa iin nts'a' hetdiik niign t'eey dzelxoh nts'ą' nii'eełts'ełe' ii'eł tah ts'exol'iik dą jah ts'ineeshyaan.

T'axoh.

we buy it for them.
That's the way we grew up,
we did not grow up like them.
Things
when we play, we copy what our mother does, that's the way we play.

We made little fish racks and we pretend that leaves are the fish and

we put them on the rack and we pretend to filet them.
All day we play, we play camp.

This is how we grew up, we didn't have it easy when we were growing up but we liked it.
We just played with anything.
We played what our mother did, we pretend to set traps, that's the way we grew up.

Enough.

Transcribed with the help of Avis and Roy Sam.

Part II

Łąy eł t'eey hutshyaak niign

Part II

Stories that really happened

8

Shnaa naholndak niign

Shnaa
ishyiit dą' k'ełt'iin teldak dą' *1912*
shnaa ntsuul.
Sheł naholndak niign ch'a dihnay.

Shnaa: nah'ogn k'ąy' ts'oo t'eey na'etk'an'.

Hugn nan' k'it t'oo niishyeey hugn t'eey na'etk'an' nts'ą'.
Kon' cho::h elo::k.
Andoo' Manh Choh shyiit t'eey dineh iin tadeltth'ih, nih.

Hugn haniign na'eełąy ay huushyiit t'eey nahdeltth'ih elogn eł.

Ch'ithüh eegąy nelgąy diitthi' k'e daheedlak nts'ą' ay shyiit hetshyih
łat ch'a łat eł hu'įįtsįį dał t'eey hǫǫłįį.
Łą' t'eey dineh iin xa hiihǫǫtsüü:: ishyiit dą'.

8

A story that Mom told

When Cora told me the story, she said that this was the 1912 Katmai eruption; it is unlikely that an eruption of Katmai would have set the Tetlin area on fire. More likely, her mother remembered the 1911 eruption of Mount Wrangell, which is significantly closer. A description of the event is available from the website of the Alaska Volcano Observatory.[1] *It was also described in the Chitina Leader.*

My mother;
when that volcano erupted in 1912,
my mother was little.[2]
I say it the way she told me stories about it.

My mother [said]; out there, the willows and the spruce even were burning.
Even things growing on the land were burning.
The fire was large and hot.
Up there in 'big lake' (Tetlin Lake), people were sitting in the water, she said.[3]
And also in the creeks flowing from everywhere they were standing in there, with the heat.
They put dried skins over their heads and breathed like that but still their noses started bleeding with the smoke.
This time was very hard for people.

Huuch'il, huushyah,
hǫ' ch'a nts'ą' t'eey hǫ' nahutk'ąą.
K'at'eey <sihohdihthanh> nts'ą' t'eey nahutk'ąą.
Nde' tah <łahtthagn nts'ą'> hįįdlą' nts'ą' thihtedeeł,
ne' <Naambia Niign'> nts'ą' ne' huunde' tah <<hidzedeeł>>.
Hihdįįtsįį eł hihteedeeł huutah dineh iin hu'ich'eh'aal ha hune'
hihteedeel łuu'.

Diniign huh udzih iin t'eey kol.
<Łahtthagn nts'ą'> nahetk'ąą.
Neetsay iin t'eey nahetk'ąą nts'ą'.
Dii t'eey kol.
Huune' tah hįįdlah nts'ą' thihteedeel eł.
Hanuugn t'iin iin <hune'> *Black Hills,* henihniik nts'ą' thihteedeeł dą'
ay iin k'e t'eey hihteedeeł huunde'.
Huugn nahutk'ąą niign huhneedeeł tąy shyįį nahuu'ah niign hodaat'įį
niign thihteedeeł.

Dii t'eey k'a nahtełeeg nts'ą'.
Dą' diihiishyįį etl'oon ayshįį eł thihteedeeł.

Nuug ishyiit huhtah dineh iin huu diniign hihdhexįį
huugn shyi' naaheedlay iin hu'ich'eh'aał nts'ą' hǫǫsu' hihdeltth'ih.
Ay t'oot'eey dineh iin hah ih'ǫǫtsüü:: nts'ą'.
Dii:: t'eey kol hultsįį.
Shnaa sheł naholndak dą' che.

K'at'eey dii t'eey ts'e'aal.
Nts'ą' nathits'eldak shįį' t'eey, nih.
Huk'aan ch'a.
Huu'įįtsįį dał t'eey naahǫǫłį' nts'ą'.
Huu t'eey
hugn ts'et'ia ii'eł k'a t'eey nih neeshin k'et.
Aba::h, hnih.
Tl'aan t'eey hiihǫǫtsüü nii t'eey dineh iin daanuutniithad ishyiit dą'.
Ay t'eey k'at'eey hiixa naholnii.
Hits'ehetniign ay eł łe'.

Their clothes, their houses,
everything burned up.
They were not prepared when that burn-out happened.
They all ran up toward the South,
They ran toward 'rippling creek' (Northway).
They were hungry and they kept running; so the [Northway] people fed them, that's why they ran there.

There were no moose, no caribou.
Everything burned.
Even the bears burned.
There was nothing left.
They all ran up that way.
The people up there [around black hills] they all went up to the Black Hills and they followed them up there.
Everything was burned where they went and where the trail extends, it was visible, that's the way they ran.

They didn't carry anything.
Only with the clothes that they were wearing they ran up.

Up there people had killed moose
and had meat; so they feed them, and they stayed pretty well.
But even so, people had it hard.
There was nothing left that you can think of.
My mother told me the story about this.

We never ate anything.
We were just running, she said.
From the burn-out.
And they had nosebleeds.
Even
our skin roasted.
It hurt, she said.
And it was very hard what happened to all these people at that time.
They never tell stories about it.
Maybe they don't know about it.

T'oot'eey shnaa hǫǫshdįįnį' t'oot'eey k'at'eey t'oot'eey hǫǫ'idihnąy.

K'ahdu'
dan ha hǫǫłįį dą' atthuugn
huugn neek'e hohdeldii ha
atthuugn tah
kon' ch'aa hihdeltth'ih dą'
dzeltth'ii eł.

Noodlee
huugn jinetl'agn huhnenee'ąą nts'ą', "Jah dugn nuhkeey <łahtthag>
huune' ahdlą' nts'ą' nuhtah hǫǫdąy t'eey k'a hǫǫdahnay,"
nee'ehnih.
"Shnaa hǫǫ shehnih t'oot'eey doo chishduutthaag ha chih,"
hǫǫdihniil.
Achąą eł t'eey chih
huuxa naahǫǫt'eh.
Achąą iin t'eey k'a naholndii.
Shnaa du' <łahtthagn nts'ą'> huugn nts'ą' hutshyaak nii t'eey sheł
naholniign nts'ą'.
Hi'ishnay.

Tuu niihąą niign t'eey sheł nahalnagn.
Ay du' <Dziin Choh saa> k'et ch'a hutshyaay huut'eey ch'a sheł
nahalndagn.
Ay xa ha' guuy nts'ą' nuh'eł nahogndagn hach'ale.
Jan hǫǫdihnay.

Ayshįį t'eey.

My mother told me, but I never told anybody.

Today
four years ago down there
at culture camp
down there
they were sitting by the open fire
we were sitting there.

A white man
brought that book and "All you people around here and you never said anything about it," he said to us.

"My mother told me but who would listen,"
I said.
Even the old people
don't care.
Even the old people don't tell stories.
My mother used to tell me stories about this long ago.

That's how I know.

She even told me about the flood.
It happened in December [lit. Christmas month], she even told me a story about that.
I'll tell you little bit about it, not all of it.
That's why I say that.

That's enough.

Transcribed with the help of Cora David.

Notes

1. http://avo.alaska.edu/volcanoes/volcact.php?volcname=Wrangell&eruptionid=444&page=basics.
2. Cora estimates that her mother was about 10 years old at the time.
3. Not just in Tetlin Lake, but in all of the larger lakes in the Tetlin area.

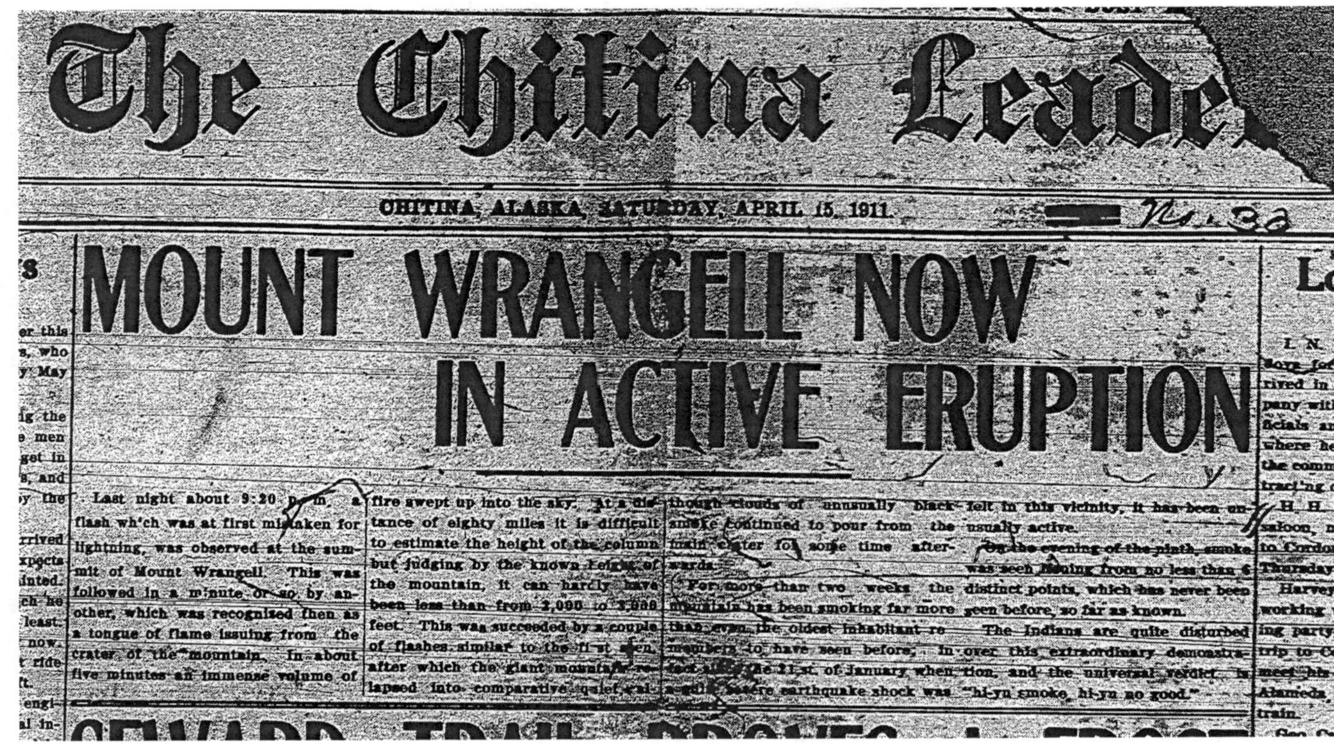

The Chitina Leader

CHITINA, ALASKA, SATURDAY, APRIL 15, 1911.

MOUNT WRANGELL NOW IN ACTIVE ERUPTION

Last night about 9:20 p. m. a flash wh'ch was at first mistaken for lightning, was observed at the summit of Mount Wrangell. This was followed in a minute or so by another, which was recognised then as a tongue of flame issuing from the crater of the mountain. In about five minutes an immense volume of fire swept up into the sky. At a distance of eighty miles it is difficult to estimate the height of the column but judging by the known height of the mountain, it can hardly have been less than from 2,000 to 3,000 feet. This was succeeded by a couple of flashes similar to the first seen, after which the giant mountain relapsed into comparative quiet, although clouds of unusually black smoke continued to pour from the main crater for some time afterwards.

For more than two weeks the mountain has been smoking far more than even the oldest inhabitant remembers to have seen before; in fact since the 21st. of January when a quite severe earthquake shock was felt in this vicinity, it has been unusually active.

On the evening of the ninth, smoke was seen issuing from no less than 6 distinct points, which has never been seen before, so far as known.

The Indians are quite disturbed over this extraordinary demonstration, and the universal verdict is "hi-yu smoke, hi-yu no good."

The Chitina Leader, "Mount Wrangell Now in Active Eruption," April 15, 1911. Microfilm. Alaska and Polar Regions Collections, Elmer E. Rasmuson Library, University of Alaska Fairbanks.

Mount Wrangell now in active eruption

The *Chitina Leader,* Chitina, Alaska, Saturday, April 15, 1911

Last night about 9:20 p.m. a flash which was at first mistaken for lightning, was observed at the summit of Mount Wrangell. This was followed in a minute or so by another, which was recognized then as a tongue of flame issuing from the crater of the mountain. In about five minutes an immense volume of fire swept up into the sky. At a distance of eighty miles it is difficult to estimate the height of the column but judging by the known height of the mountain, it can hardly have been less than from 3,000 to 8,000 feet. This was succeeded by a couple of flashes, similar to the first seen, after which the giant mountain relapsed into comparative quiet and though clouds of unusually black smoke continued to pour from the usually main crater for some time afterwards.

For more than two weeks the mountain has been smoking far more than even the oldest inhabitant remembers to have seen before; in fact, since the 21st of January, when a quite severe earthquake was felt in this vicinity, it has been unusually active.

On the evening of the ninth, smoke was seen issuing from no less than [6?] distinct points, which has never been seen before, so far as known.

The Indians are quite disturbed over this extraordinary demonstration, and the universal verdict is "hi-yu smoke, hi-yu no good."

9

Shnaa nee'eł naholndak tuu niihaan xa

Nahk'ade dą'
shnaa iin hįįtsuul eł
<Dihthaad> dą' hihteenaa,
hihteneeyh.
<T'axoh t'eey> hihteenaan eł t'eey chih
nohdįą nahatdal.

Nahk'ade nts'ą' nahatdal eł t'eey
tuu nii'oo skeniihaan.
Manh Choh ts'an *all through that place*
tuu skeniihąą.
Tuu niihąą <hiiyehnih>.

9

Mom told us about the flood

Here, Cora describes the Great Flood that happened in Last Tetlin in the early 20th century. Her mother was born in 1902, and was still a child. Cora highlights the importance of being prepared, and of having survival skills.

This is one of the first stories that Cora told me. Because she knew I had a hard time following her when she spoke in her language, she used quite a lot of English.

At 'fish trap' (Last Tetlin)
my parents were little
they went off to 'nearby place' (Tanacross)
they were going to move.
They had already moved there
and they were moving back.

They moved back to 'fish trap' and
water was all over.
From 'big lake' (Tetlin Lake) onward,
there was water all over.
Flood, they call it.

Nahk'ade nahindeel eł jah ndee k'it dahtaadał <łahtthagn nts'ą'> huushyah shyiit tuu.

Shnaa huugn t'eey ch'a sheł naholndak
uxa huhshyąh xa.

K'ahdu'
nanetshyeey iin jah k'ahdu' ts'iikeey,
t'siikeey iin huugn t'eey ch'a huu'ahdaaniil.

Ddhał eekeh
nahindeeł tl'aan hugn nahteedak nts'ą' jah ndee k'it nihtaadał.
Hanadegn Nahk'ade hanadegn ddhał eekeh
łat hihneh'įh,
łat ta'įį'ah.
Ishyiit nts'ą' hihteedeeł eł ishyiit tah,
ishyiit nts'ą' hihteedeeł eł t'eey ishyiit dą' nihniinąą nts'ą' diishyah huugn niimbaal shyah hihxaan ay shyiit hihdeltth'ix.

Neenaattheh dą' neh hugn ch'a ishyiit neeshyaan.

Ay shyiit ishyiit nihneedeel eł:
"Tsin'įį! Neeshyah <łahtthagn nts'ą'> tuu daatneehaan eł t'eey ch'a shyah udhahtsiin," henih.
"Jah chih nuhshyah ts'ehutsiin," nih. "Jah tah tidhaltth'ix," <hu'ehnih>.

Stsay Chief Luke <nts'ą'> u'aat, shnaa, shnaa ts'iiniin nłįįn eł t'eey.

Huugn ch'a
nuhts'iikeey atdahniil.
Hǫǫxutshyąą dahniil nts'ą'.

"Shyah suu shyiit didhaltth'ih nts'ą'
nuhxa hǫǫsǫǫ, "<neenih>.
"Thee' de'!

When they got to 'fish trap', there was no place where they could land,
all their homes were in the water.

My mother told me this
so I get smart.

Today,
the new generation, the children today,
you guys have to tell the children.

Halfway up the mountain
they came back and there was too much water to land.
Up there by 'fish trap' (Last Tetlin), halfway up the mountain
they saw smoke,
smoke was visible.
They started to go there and there,
they went up there and they made camp there; they made shelters and
they stayed there.

Long before us, they grew up in places like that.

When they got there:
"Thank you. Our house is full of water, and you made a shelter for us,"
they said to them.
"We made you guys' house too," they said. "So you can just stay
there," they told them.
My grandpa Chief Luke, his wife, my mother was still a child.

Things like that
you guys should teach that to your children.
You'll teach them so they'll be smart.

"You guys live in a nice house and
you like it," she told us.
"Just wait!

Nuhshyah eł tuu niihąą de', k'at'eey nuhshyah suu utaałeel.

Ndugn tahdał tah hahdogn,
nuhts'adn, diitah'aal eł diishyii' tahtiadn eł nuhch'il eł da'ahtlaak
shyiit," nee'ehnih.

Eli:h.
<Huuxa nijelnay,>
k'at'eey <łahtthagn nts'ą'> k'a hitanh nts'ą' hǫǫsu' nts'ą' t'eey
huushyah huhǫǫhxąą nihihdeltth'ih anadog ddhał eekeh.

Ishyiit deltth'ii iin ch'a
jah dineh deltth'ii iin huuk
tsaa tah haahiłeek nts'ą' nadogn ishyiit niihiiyelshyeek.

In the event that your house is flooded, you won't have a nice home any longer.
When you go somewhere,
put your blankets, your food, what you're going to sleep in and your clothes, in a high place," she said to us.

It was cold.
They were lucky,[1]
that they didn't all freeze to death, and it was good that
they were staying in the house that people had made for them halfway up the mountain.
The people staying there
the people staying there
they're digging into their caches and there they bring food back.

Transcribed with the help of Avis and Roy Sam.

Notes

1. *Literally:* someone had mercy on them.

⁓ 10 ⁓

Ts’iit Tl’oo Ddhal’ xa nahogndak

Ts’iit Tl’oo.

Ay chih ch’ale’
ahtthugn, ahtthugn nts’ą’
Toochinh nts’ą’ nahatdał tah
hii’aa’an ch’uutnel’ii:k tah
ha guuy nts’ą’ hooniign t’eey detth’iik yahiidegn ddhał tthiit’aagn nts’ą’.
Ddhał tthiit’aag nts’ą’ <<ch’uudehshyaa k’eh niik, >> “Oooooooo” ndiik.
Ishyiit tah dǫǫ ehts’ayy’ choh t’eey ha’ehaak
nts’ą’
dineh iin niitanh dulthii kah t’eey
diik,
hǫǫdiik <nts’ą’> nahdǫǫ natetdak tah *or* jah ts’an nahtthan natetdak ch’a du hǫǫdiik.

K’at’eey hii’aa’an hii’uudagn.

10

I talk about 'porcupine grass mountain'

This narrative is a good illustration of the Tetlin people's relationship to the landscape as something to interact with.

'Porcupine grass [mountain]'.

As for that, too
coming from down there
when they're coming back from 'sticks in water' (Midway Lake),
when they try to sneak by
he hears every little noise they make, from on top of that hill.

At the top of the hill, he makes a whistling sound, he says
"Oooooooooo."
And then the north wind comes really strongly
and
he even tries to freeze people
in this way,
he does that when they come from down there and when they go down
[from Tetlin] he does that.

They never pass him.

Hii'aa'an hi'uteedaak tah
k'at'ee::y
shaheh'aag nts'ą' k'at'eey nts'ą::' t'eey hidiig nts'ą' ch'ihnel'iik
    hii'aa'an ch'uunel'iik shįį',
t'oot'eey
dineh iin hii'aa'an utetdak tah
shaheh'aag *or* nahuugn
hudelxoł tah t'eey
detth'iik nts'ą'.
Hǫǫndii "guuuuuuu" nii nts'ą' <<ch'uudetshyaay k'eh ndiig nts'ą'>>.
Dǫǫ ehts'ayy' ha'ehhaag nts'ą'
shyüh eł t'eey hohdiit.
Elii::h, <chih>
dineh uktanh xa.

Stsay, stsǫǫ Martha <<Luke>> uta';
hutǫǫ huuhetdąy eł t'eey hutǫǫ nahatdal eł t'eey.

Nadeg nts'ą' <ch'uudchshyaa>.
Stsay huudegn nts'ą'
na'ethat nts'ą':
"Jah ts'an noo'
huhnay noo' t'eey k'a hǫǫnatdindiil," iiyehnih.
Yih etshyinh.
Stsay etshyinh eł t'eey
k'a t'eey hǫǫt'eey nadetnay nts'ą' t'eey.
Hǫǫt'eey k'ahdu' dziin t'eey k'a hǫǫt'eey nadetnay.

Dii le' nay huh.
Hutthiit'aagn natihdaag tat'eey k'at'eey dii t'eey nak'ąy dii le'.
Dii le' ch'a hǫǫndiik henąy.

When they try to pass him
not
they don't make a noise and they don't do anything and they sneak by and sneak by,
but
when people go by him
they make noise or up there
even when they just play around
he hears it.
He says "Guuuuuuuu," and makes a sound like a whistle.
The north wind comes and
even a snow blizzard.
It is cold, too
so he can freeze people.

My grandfather, the father of my grandmother Martha Luke;
they were coming back from down there, they were walking back from down there.
He whistled up there.
My grandfather up there
stood up [toward that hill]:
"From now on
from now on and here on, you will not say this again," he said to him.
He made medicine.
My grandfather made medicine and
he stopped making that whistling sound.
Up to this day, he has not made that whistling sound again.

I don't know what it is.
I went right on top of it, but I saw nothing.
I wonder what it is that made a noise like that.

Transcribed and translated with the help of Cora David.

Martha Luke in Tetlin. Tetlin Photograph Collection, UAF-1987-0114-43, Alaska and Polar Regions Collections, Elmer E. Rasmuson Library, University of Alaska Fairbanks.

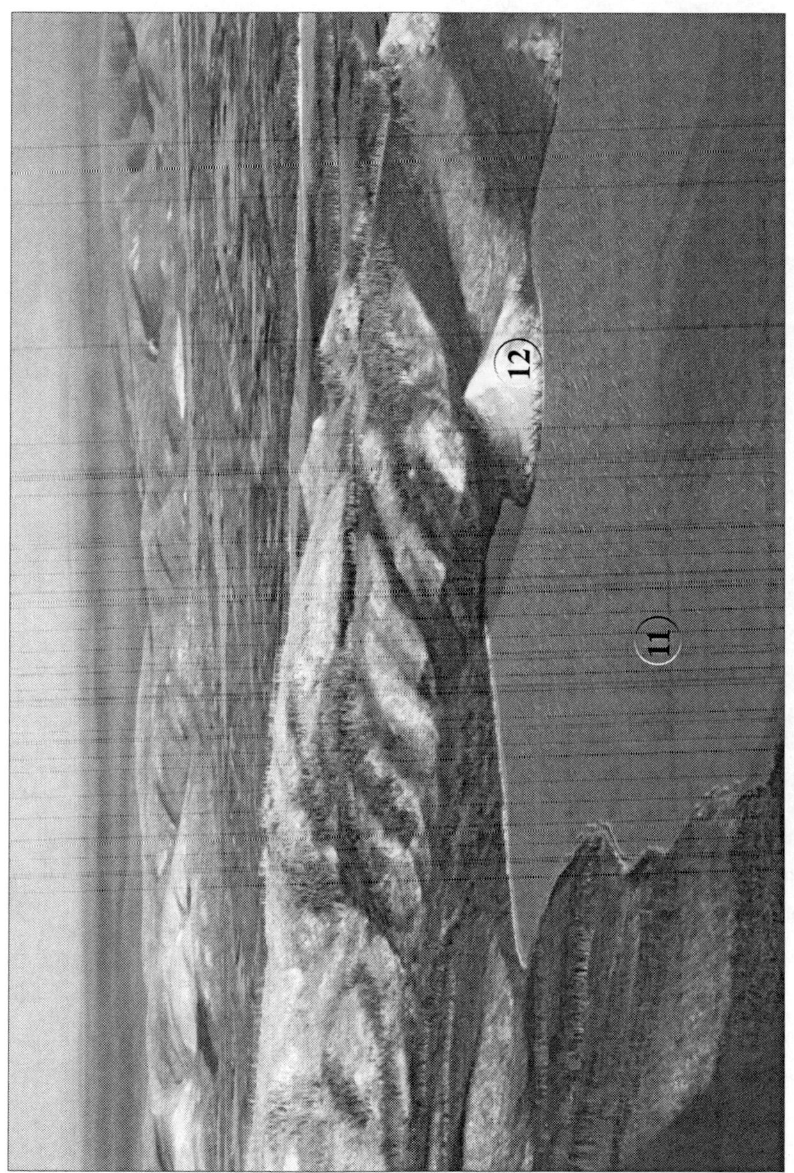

Porcupine Grass Lake (Ts'iit Tl'oo Mann', 11) and Porcupine Grass Mountain (Ts'iit Tl'oo Ddhal', 12).

~ 11 ~

Ts'ist'e' diichaay iin eł nahembaa iin k'ii hitdeeł

Neenaattheh dą'
ts'ist'e'
<<uchaay łaakey iin elt'eh>>.
Diichaay iin dehtth'ii.

Eł
huukąy' iin <łahtthagn nts'ą'>
huukąy' iin nahdogn
nahelseey xa stahnideeł.
Huugn
dineh iin
ts'exeh iin ts'ist'e' hihdelttth'ih.
<Teedląy> keey yanagdegn
nadegn tąy hǫǫłįį, shįį tąy.
Hudegn
jign kah hihteedeel eł
jign hihnehtsayh tl'aan
nohdįą' nahatdał na'įhxeel eł.

11

The old lady and her granddaughters met with warriors

This is an account of a war that took place a long time ago.

Long before us
an old lady
had two grandchildren.
Her grandchildren were staying with her.

And
all of their husbands
their husbands on the side of the hill
they went out hunting.
Right there
people
the girls and the old lady are sitting around.
In 'current flows' (Tetlin) village, going up there
up there there is a trail.[1]
Up that way
they went to look for blueberries and
they were picking berries and then
they came back the same way when it was getting evening.

Naadegn nts'ą'
ts'oo t'aat
hihdeltth'ih tl'aan nee' no' shiign hohneh'į̨.
Ch'its'aa' hultsį̨.
"Ch'its'aa' t'eey hotdį'," hutsǫǫ hu'ehni t'oot'eey
ts'exeh gaay iin du', "Neekąy' iin hihdelxoo ay nts'ą' hanteey'
natsutdeel!"
Dineh hehxaan iin tth'i k'iiheet'üü ay nahdelkagn eł hihdelxoo.

Ts'exeh iin
anoo' shiign naakąą hihtelshyah, huutsǫǫ:
"Hanaann'
"tsiił tüh sketidhahdeeł de' nuh'eegn degn,
"ts'exeh iin ahłį̨ <<nts'ą'>>
"ishyiit de'
"k'a nuhhihdaxaan," hu'ehni.

Hunaann' tsiił k'etdaheedeeł nts'ą'
hantee:y' nahatdał
hanteey' nahatdał nts'ą'
hohneh'ąy eł
dineh iin hihdelxoo:::
dineh tthi' eł.
Daheedeeł <nts'ą'>
k'at'eey hahniidal.
Huu'eł
hunaann' daheedeel eł dii'eegn degn huundayh
ay eł ts'exeh hį̨łį̨ nts'ą' huhneh'ąy eł.
"Ayt'oo
"nee'eł hihtuudeel," huuhinih.

Huunaagn' k'e ch'ehudehchüh tl'aan
ne' nahuuteedlah.

Up on the hillside
under a spruce
they were sitting and were looking down.
It looked different.
"Everything is different," their grandmother told them but
the young girls: "Our boyfriends[2] are playing and we want to go down
there, hurry up!"
They killed men and cut their heads off; then they played ball with [the
heads].

The girls
they ran down the hill, their grandmother:
"Going across
"when you go across the bridge, pull your dress up,
"[so they can see that] you are girls
"there
"so they don't kill you guys," she told them.

They got to the bridge to walk over to the other side
they're walking back in a hurry
they're walking back in a hurry and
they are looking
the men are playing
with people's heads.
They walk right on [that bridge]
they didn't turn around.
With them
they got on the bridge and they pulled up their dresses
so that they can see that they're girls.
"All right
"they have to go with us," they said to them.

They blindfolded them and
took them down south.

Nduu huuhaałeeł niign t'eey k'a hihitnayh.
Ch'aadeh
ch'aadeh du'
huugn
tsat huugn t'eey
hohnuh'įį xa huugn <<mbah iin>>
diike' eł t'eey
dlaat shyiit etak nts'ą'
mbah iin hohnuh'įį xa
hishyah hoodįht-'įį.
Huugn k'ąy' t'eey tah nde' tatneetsak nee' hadał niik.
Nduu hatdał ts'ą' k'at'eey hihitnąy, huunaagn'
huunaagn' k'e ch'ehuudehchüü eł.

Nee::' nahatdał,
ndiit
mbah
manh choh <yihinih>
manh choh
ay maagn nihniideeł eł.

Diishyah
ch'ithüh shyah hoohuutsįį, "ay shyiit nats'ulshyii nts'ą' jah dzaltth'iił
tl'aan jah ts'ahtiat," huuhinih.
<< "Nuhk'aa' thüh danahłeeł uk'it nats'oonuukąą xa natl'ade eł.">>
Ch'ithüh shyah shyiit dahuuneedlay eł
daadeh eł ishyiit dahuuneedlah.
Udia' xǫǫshyąą.
"Huuk'aa' k'it nats'oonuukąą ay neexa dahuułeey dą'"
nih.

Eł t'eey nah'ogn nts'ą' moondaa
hǫǫheyh.

They didn't know where they took them.
The older sister
the older sister
around
even wood
so the warriors could see
with their feet
they put their feet down hard in the moss
so warriors could see
there was a sign where they went.
They twisted willows too as they were walking south.
They don't know where they're walking, their eyes
they had blindfolded them.

They went way down south
way back
the warriors
to what they call ocean
ocean
they came to the shore.

Their houses
they made teepees and, "We'll rest inside and we will stay here and
sleep," they tell them.
"Bring in all your gun cases so we can sew beads on them."
They put it all in the teepee and
she and her older sister took them all inside.
That younger sister is smart.
"Bring it in to us so we can sew on their guns,"
they said.

And outside her older brother
he was talking.

Didia' eł daadeh eł uusih nts'ą'
"Jah nits'iniideeł!" eł "Oh! Shoondaa!" nih
ay eł udia'.
Hahnaat dineh tth'i'elt'ayh hǫ'
dineh ishyiit eedah nts'ą'
nahu'udah'įį.
"Nday! Nts'aa' hutshyaak?"
"Ch'ikol!
"Doondaa k'et ts'ihǫǫdąy," hatnih.

Ay eł
natehxeel eł
huuk'aa' huu'eł dahełeey
iik'it natl'ade eł naach'ihnaakąą xa.
<Łahtthagn nts'ą'> dahiiniidlah nts'ą'
diishyah shyiit huushyah shyiit dahiiniidlay eł.

"Duka'!
"Nee' natidhahdeel de'
"sǫ' sǫ' ni'ahdag nts'ą'
"altthał nts'ą' <łahtthagn nts'ą'>
"hantee:y' t'eey
"altthał nts'ą'
"k'at'eey nitahhaagn nts'ą'.
"Nihthaa:d ninahdeeł de' tah
"na'alshyiih de',"
huu'oondah hu'ehnih.

Hǫǫ hetdįį hǫǫhetshyaak
gąą halshyeeł
eł
nahugn
<ay shyiit gąą halshyah.
Tthee shyiit ch'ii'anh hǫǫłįį dą'.>
Hehtiat.

He called the younger sister and the older sister and:
"We came here," and "Oh! My older brother!" she said,
the younger sister.
Over there a man was lying
a man was sitting inside [the same tent] and
he looked at them.
"What! What happened?"
"Nothing!
"She misses her older brother," she said.

And
in the evening
they brought in their guns
so they could sew beads on them.
They brought them all in and
they brought them all into the house.

"Okay!
"When you walk back
"don't wait
"keep on running and all
"hurry up
"keep on running and
"you can't stop.
"When you get far away
"take a rest."
their older brother said to them.

They did as he had told them
they ran to a cave
and
back there
they ran into a cave.
There was a cave in the rocks.
They slept.

Hǫǫt'eey hehtiadn eł denuugn
huumǫǫndaa iin dineh iin <łahtthagn nts'ą'> hįįxąą.
Huuhįįxąą.
Ishyiit
ts'ehłagn dineh
huugn łuugn eldeel ay ajettsat nts'ą' noo' tah
ambeeł nts'ą'.
Hiyuhdiih t'oot'eey huk'e'
ts'ehtąy'
<huk'e'> na'etdeeyh.
Ts'ehtąy' eł hiiyuhdiih nts'ą'
dichin' k'a' uk'e' na'etdeeyh ay.
Łuugn eldeel du'
taguuł mǫǫsį'.
"Guuł, guuł!" <nih>.

Doo iin ishyiit hu'exaan ay iin
ay iin ch'a
noo' tah
<manh choh> shyiit
manh choh shyiit ta'ambeeł.
Ay shiin t'eey huuts'an <etshyih>
k'at'eey
<łahtthagn nts'ąh> hįłak.
Huhįįxąą toot'eey <ts'ehłag> ayshįį hǫǫndayh.

Ayshįį t'eey.

While they were sleeping up that way
their older brothers they killed all the men.
They killed them.
There
one man
turned himself into one of these birds that eat fish and away
he swam.
They shot at it, but following him
the arrow
it didn't go far enough.
They shoot an arrow
and the arrow fell short.
The [bird] that eats fish
taguuł[3] is his name.
"Guuł, guuł!" he says.

The ones that they killed
those ones
way out
in the ocean
it swam out in the ocean.
He's the only one that got saved,
not
all the others died.
They killed them, but one of them survived.

That's all.

Transcribed and translated with the help of Cora David.

Notes

1. The trail leading from Tetlin to Tetlin Hill. It still is there today.
2. *Neekąy'* can be translated as 'our husbands' or 'our boyfriends'.
3. Cora describes the bird as loon-like, but the word she uses is not one of the usual words for the different species of loon.

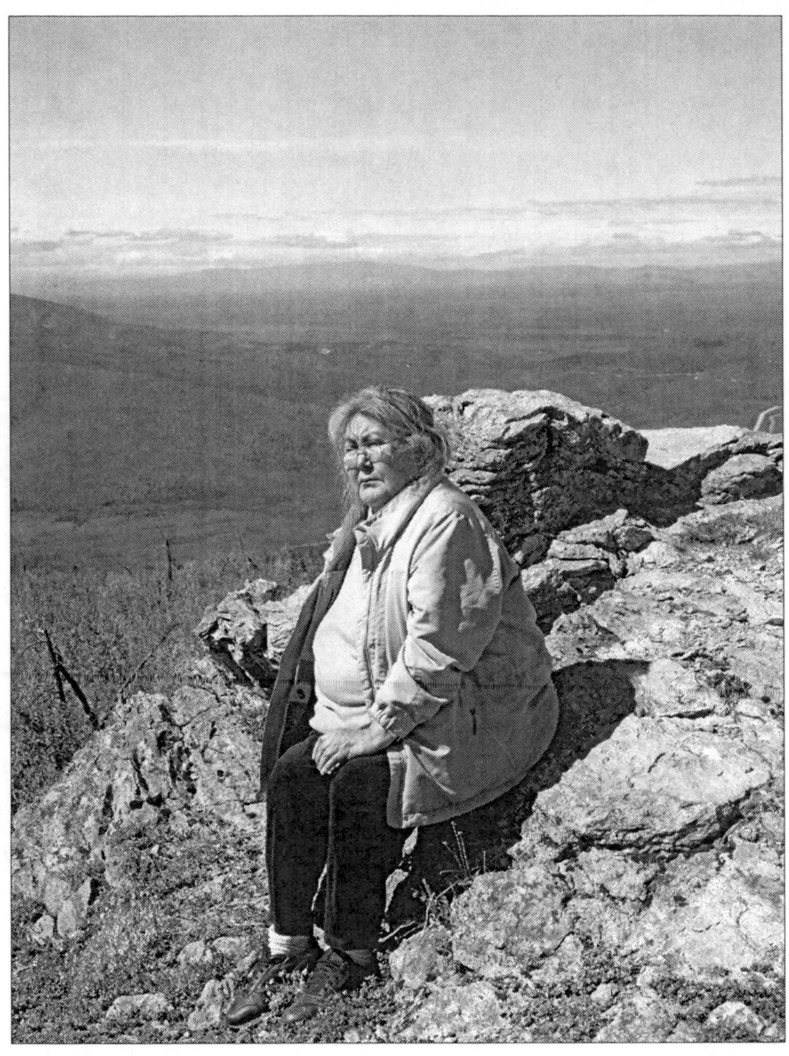

Cora David on Tetlin Hill (Teedląy Ddhal', 8). © Olga Lovick, June 2008.

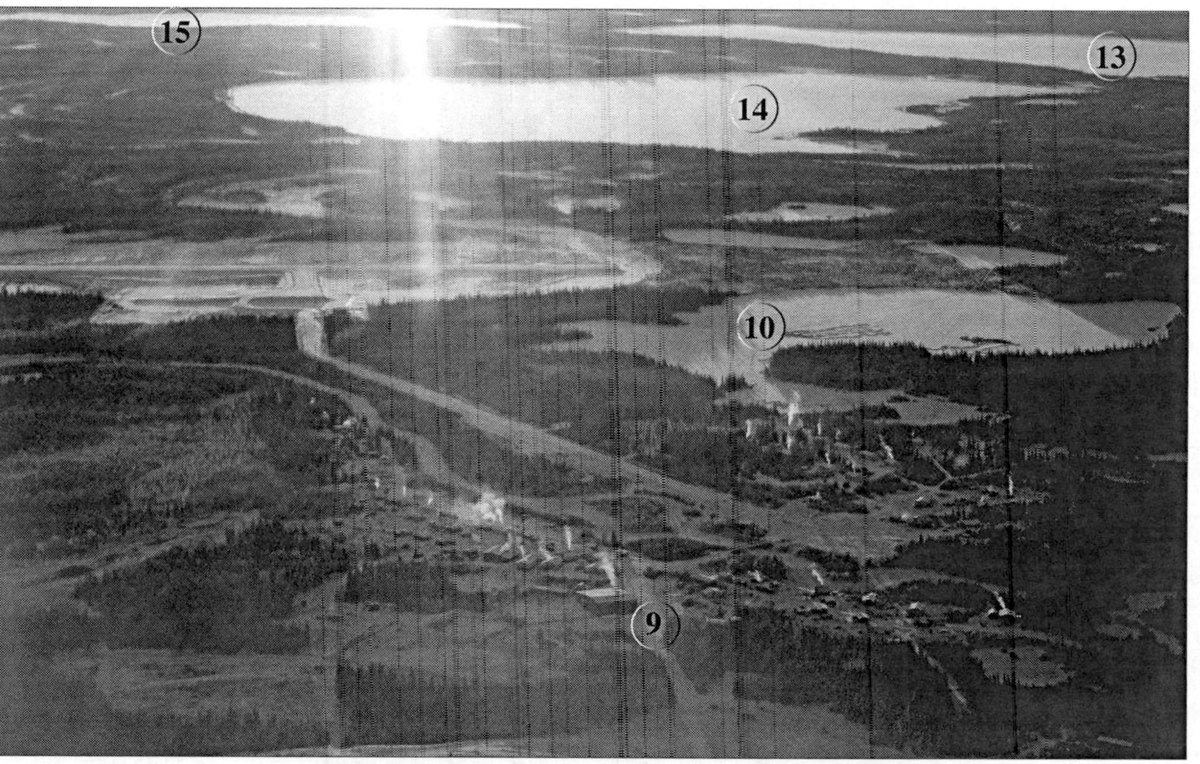

A south-facing aerial view of Tetlin (Teedlą̨y Keey, 9), Skate Lake (Tl'oh Oogn Mann', 10), Dathlamund Lake (Daałal Mann', 13), Gasoline Lake (Goo Choh Mann', 14), and Old Albert Lake (Tinii'ah Mann', 15). Photo © Jessica Cherry and Forest Kirst, December 2010.

12

Che' t'iin xa nahogndak

Neenaattheh dą'
dineh iin
huuche' ts'eegn nahǫǫłįh.
Che' t'iin
huu'ǫǫsi'.
Naatayhneetkayh dą' <Teedląy>.
Yaadaatii Naatayhneetkayh dą' ishyiit ch'a hihdaltth'ih.
Dineh iin texąą tl'aan < huuheldeeł>.
<Nasaha'aal nts'ą' > dixoh eł nihetdak tüh.

Dineh iin k'at'eey hiihitnąy Che' t'iin <<hįįłįį nts'ą'>>.

Dineh iin
łaakey iin
nahelseeyh eł hihteedeel.
Huukol.
Huukol. "Nday <<ch'a>> dineh iin <<nahelseey iin>> nahutdeeł ch'a?" hinih.
Dineh <ts'ehłagn> xǫǫshyaan huukah; huuk'eh teeshyah nts'ą' hukah

hach'udal'įį.
Che' t'iin iin xǫǫhushyąą.

12

I talk about the Tailed People

This is one of the first stories Cora told me. It is one of several accounts of tailed people in Alaska, and clearly a scary story. We talked about the story many times, and Cora kept adding detail. As a result, this is the most heavily edited story in this collection.

Long before our time
people
with a long tail existed.
Tailed People
was their name.
At 'bare hill' in 'current flows' (Tetlin).
Down there at 'bare hill', that's where they used to live.
They used to kill people, and they ate them.
Before sundown they all gathered to play.

People didn't know that there were Tailed People.

Men
two of them
went off to hunt.
They disappeared.
They disappeared. "Where are the men that went hunting?" they said.

One man figured them out; he went out following their tracks and for them
he looked around.
The Tailed People were smart.

Dineh iin nduu nahtetdak ndiik t'eey hihetndąy nts'ą' t'eey.

Ogn tąy k'üü tah anatetdaak.[1]

The following bit was inserted on August 13, 2009:

Dineh łaakey iin
huuk'eh hohna'iil ch'a',
diik'eh
nde' nts'ą' diik'eh natetdak.

Ishyiit tah "Noo' hihniideeł," huunih nts'ą' noo' tah huukah hohnee'iik.
Ne' nts'ą' du',
k'a hohneh'iign,
"Huhnoo' hihniideeł," huunih eł.

The original narrative resumes here:

K'at'eey tąy natetdak nts'ą' nah'ogn <<tąy k'üü tah natetdak>>.
He found out Che' t'iin
ay iin ch'a dineh ehxaan <<dą'>>.

Ay
<k'at'eey che' t'iin iihitnay ishyiit dą
shnaa nee'eł naholndak Che' t'iin iin xa.
"Uche' ts'eegn hǫǫłįį," nee'ehnih.
Dineh heldeeł.>

Ay t'eey ch'a dineh xǫǫshyaan
huuk'eh natetdak nts'ą'
na'inshyay eł.

They knew where people had walked.

He walked alongside the trail.

The following bit was inserted on August 13, 2009:

The two men
whose tracks he was looking for,
their tracks
were leading upstream.

There: "They went upriver!" he said and he looked for them upriver.
Upstream though,
he didn't look for them.
"They went upriver," he said to them.

The original narrative resumes here:

He didn't walk on the trail, he walked alongside the trail.
He found out that the Tailed People
kill people.

And
they didn't know monkeys in those days
[but] my mother told us that the Tailed People were like that.
"They had a long tail," she said to us.
They eat people.

And that smart man
walking around following them
he came back out.

“Nah’og dineh iin <łahtthagn> nts’ą’ hihdetshyoh nts’ą’
“huuche’ ts’eegn hǫǫłįį iin ch’a dineh <<iin>> ehxaan dą’,” nih.
“Ndee niihuuhelshyeek?”
“Datthi’ Naatayhneetkayh dą’ ch’a ishyiit ch’a huukeey na’.”
“<Teedląy> dą’ adandegn
“<<Tl’oh Oogn Mann’ dą’>>
“k’at’eey hunishyeey niig huug ch’a huukeey dą’,”
dą’ nih dineh.
Ay eł “Nts’ą’ hi’indąy ch’a dįįnay?” hiiyehnih.
“Huuk’eh natihdaa nts’ą’ huunak-’įį.
“<K’a t’eey ehts’ayh ch’ąą natihdaak nts’ą’ hunak-’įį.>
“Ay xa ch’a huu’ii’ishnąy dą’,”
dineh iin ehnih.
“<Łahtthagn nts’ą’> huuts’uuxaan!”
nih nts’ą’.

Dineh iin hǫǫ’ehnąy eł natthadn Naatayhneetkayh nts’ą’ hihtetdeeł.
<<Ch’itth’ąy eł tl’oh eł niłtah nihneedlah tl’aan huu’an shyiit hiyeedlah.>>
Łat eł kon’ eł <huhįk’ąą>.
Łat eł kon’ eł huu’hįįxąą <łahtthagn nts’ą’>.
<Jah nts’ą’ hutshyaak nts’ą’ k’a hiits’itnąy hohundąy le’ nts’ą’ niiłaag le’.>

Notes

1. Cora explained that the *Che’ t’iin iin* walk backward, so one needs to follow their tracks backward. They also put grass over their tracks to hide them.

"Out there there are men that are hairy all over and
they have long tails; they're the ones that kill people," he said.
"Where do they put them?"
"Down there in 'dried-up hill' in there is their village.
"Up there by 'current flows' (Tetlin),
"right by 'among the grass lake' (Skate Lake)
"where nothing grows, there's their village,"
said the man.
And, "How do you know what you're saying?" they asked him.
"I followed their tracks and I watched them.
"I walked out of the wind, and I watched them.
"That's how I know them,"
he said to the people.
"We will kill them all off!"
he said.

He spoke to the people and then they went to 'dried-up hill'.
They mixed fire starter fungus with dry grass and put it into the holes.

They burnt them with smoke and fire.
They killed them all with smoke and fire.
To this day, we do not know if they were dead or alive.

Transcribed and translated with the help of Cora David.

13

Deeł xa nahogndak

Deeł.

<<Ishyiit dą’>> ahnoo’ ts’ist’e’ eł
ts’exeh gaay eł dihiishįį’ hihdeltth’ih.
Ch’ithüh shyah shyiit
ishyiit hutah hihdeltth’i’ eł t’eey adoog nts’ą’ ts’iikeey <<iin>> sha’eh’ąą,
hihdelxoh.

Ts’iiniin tinih’a’ nts’ą’ “Adoog ts’iikeey dii’eł delxoo nih’įįhi,” ts’iiniin ehnih.
Ts’exeh gaay
shits’ą’ teeshyah.
Deeł ugaay eł hihdelxoo hit’aa tihiiyetthak adogn di.
Dahiyihchik degn tay t’aa tihiiyehtthak.
Ts’exeh gaay dayihshił nts’ą’ di’eek t’aa yįxał’ą diitsǫǫ nts’ą’ nateltthat.

13

I talk about cranes

This story is a classic and exists in several Alaskan Athabascan groups. It is a classical lesson story about the proper treatment of animals.

Cranes.

At that time, an old lady
and a little girl were staying out there all by themselves.
In a teepee
they were sitting and the children over there were making a lot of noise,
they were playing,

She sent the child out and "Look what the kids over there are playing with," she said to the child.
The girl
went over there.
They were playing with a baby crane, throwing it high up in the air.
They caught it and threw it up again.
The girl caught the crane and threw it under her skin shawl and ran back to her grandmother.

<Ay eł> diitsǫǫ "Dii ch'a hiiyeh'ąy?"
Ts'exeh gaay du': "Deeł gaay ch'ale hiiyeh'ąy!"
<Ay eł>
ts'ist'e':
"Tsat <łahtthag nts'ą'> nah'ogn nitnįįłeeł!"
"Dii xa tihdiil?"
"Tahshyüü:: hukah.
"Hihtaałaa, dineh iin ts'iikeey iin <łahtthag nts'ą'> hihtaałaa.
"Łahtthag nts'ą' hihtaałaa."

<<Nts'ą' utsǫǫ yehnay niign dii,>> tsexeh gaay tsat niidelshyeek, tsat niidelshyeek.
Ishyiit hihdelxoo iin du' k'at'eey nts'ą' deehetdąy.
Deeł hadogn' sts'aakenaat'ah ntsa' jeh'ąą.
Ay eł
utsǫǫ': "Nahdog deeł sts'akenaat'aa jeh'aan dįįtth'ak!

"K'a shąąnąy, tahshyüü:.
"Ay xa tnih."

Ay eł
ay eł t'eey ehshyüh ehshyüh ehshyüh nts'ą'

And her grandmother: "What are they playing with?"
The girl: "They're playing with a baby crane!"
And
the old lady:
"Bring all the wood outside!"[1]
"Why should I do that?"
"Because it is going to snow.
"They will die; the people, the children, they are all going to die.
"They are all going to die."

Just as her grandmother had told her, the girl brought in wood, brought in wood.
The ones that had been playing didn't do anything.
A crane was circling overhead and she was singing.[2]
And
the grandmother: "You listen to that crane circling overhead and singing!
"It doesn't do it for nothing, it's going to snow.
"That's why she's singing."

And
and then it snowed and snowed and snowed and

dineh iin nah'ogn deltth'ii iin
k'at'eey huushi' t'eey huułay nts'ą' <łahtthag nts'ą'> hįįłak łahtthag
nts'ą' t'eey hįįłag.
<Łahtthag nts'ą'> ts'iikeey iin t'eey łahtthag nts'ą' naahįįłaak nts'ą'.
<Łahtthag nts'ą'> nahįįłaak nts'ą'.

<<Łahtthag nts'ą' jahtthak!>>
Jah
nts'ą' dihnay ay
uxa ts'ehuushyą' xa ch'ale neeheenay.
"Nah'ogn
"ts'ugaay eł
"diniign *whatever* nah'ogn
"sǫ' meh dalxoo," <neehinih>.

the people that had stayed outside
they had no food, they all died, all of them died.

All the children died, all of them.
All of them died.

You all listen to the story!
This
I say this
so we become smart; that's why they tell us.
"Out there
"birds and
"moose, whatever out there
"don't play with it," they used to tell us.

Transcribed and translated with the help of Cora David.

Notes

1. The old lady is telling her granddaughter to stack firewood all around the teepee for insulation and heating.
2. The crane is making medicine. Cora's mother still knew the song that the crane was singing, but Cora does not remember it.

Part III

Ts’exuushyąąk niign

Part III

Stories how we can become smart

14

Nedzeegn xa nahogndak

Jan Nedzeegn ha'.
Nak'eet doodįįłįį
neenaattheh dą'.
Neenaattheh dą' uxa ts'exushyąą ch'a nee'eł nahoholniik.

Ts'ist'e' diits'iikeey, ts'exeh gaay iin eł
dogn tah hihdeltth'ih.
Łaakeey ts'exeh gaay shįį' uudehtth'ih.
Eł natehxak tah ts'iiniin etsaa:: hihdehtth'ik hah'ogn nts'ą'.
Hiikah tetdak tah ch'ikol.
"Ukah unah'įį," huu'ehniik tah.
Hah'ogn hiikah nanetaak dą' k'at'eey hiyuudih'aay.
Taagn dą' hiikah tineedeel t'oot'eey k'at'eey hiiyudih'aal.

14

I talk about Nedzeegn

Cora told this story in installments, first a segment in English and then in her language. The recording begins with the first segment in her language but contains the second and third segments in both languages.

She translates the name of the boy, Nedzeegn, as 'yucky face' or 'half face'. Roy and Avis Sam, who helped transcribe this story, said the name reminded them of the word ch'aldzeegn *'moon'. Cora did not agree with them.*

This is the story of Nedzeegn.
This happened
long before us.
They used to tell us stories of long before our time to make us smart.

An old lady and her children, girls
were living way over there.
Just two girls were staying with her.
When it got dark, they could hear a baby crying outside somewhere.
They went looking for him, but found nothing.
"Go look for him," [the old lady] told [the girls].
They went looking out there for him but couldn't find him.
They went looking for him three times, but couldn't find him.

Dan dą' etsaa eł
huutsǫǫ "Shin tah hukah honuk'įį.
"Sǫ' shk'eh tahdeel," huu'ehnih.
Iikah an tiniishyah nts'ą' yikah natetdagn eł
yudih'ąą ts'oo daatagn ǫǫtah ha'įįt'ay.
Ts'iiniin guu::y etsaa::.
Ch'aydihtįį tlaad thüh
ts'at guuy ehtsįį eł yina'udetluh tl'aan
tay teltįį dayiltįį.

Ts'iiniin gaay
hanteey t'eey neeshyąą dineh choh eltsįį.
Nedzeegn hiiyehnih.
Nts'ąą' utsǫǫ yehnih tah ch'its'ąą shįį t'eey dį'.

"Hah'ogn łigaay
"gąął tah natinłuuk," yehnih.
Łigaay thiin tl'uuł nineedlah tl'aan
uk'eh naytetdak eł
łigaay thiich'ehchüh naytet-łuugn eł.
Łigaay ehtįį.
Diitsǫǫ haniyiltįį, "T'axo' ch'ale
"naanishłuu!"
diitsǫǫ ehnih.
"Hǫǫ laa ndihnih ha'!
"Hah'ogn natįįdaak deeł beeł eł natįįlteek ch'a ndihnay k'a hǫǫ dhįxeh natinłuug k'a ndihnay," yehnih.

Ay eł
"Aadogn gah kah dach'įįtl'uh," yehnih.
Ahdogn ts'oo k'it tah dach'itl'uh nts'ą' tsugaay iin <łahtthagn nts'ą'> huugn iitah nah'etlǫǫ nts'ą' tsugaay iin na'eet'ayh.
Hehłaagn eł.

The fourth time he was crying and
their grandmother said, "Me, I'm going to look for him.
"Don't follow me," she said to them.
She went outside to look for him and
she found him lying between two spruce trees.
The little baby was crying.
she picked him up, skin
he was wrapped in a little (skin) blanket and
she brought him back into her house.

The little baby
grew up pretty fast, he became a big man.
Nedzeegn ('half face') was his name.
Whatever his grandma told him, he did the opposite.

"Outside the puppy
drag him around the snare line," she said to him.
She put a rope around the puppy's neck and
it was walking behing him and
he choked the puppy, dragging it.
The puppy died.
He dragged it to his grandmother, "That's it,
"I dragged him back!"
he said to his grandmother.
"I didn't tell you that!
"I told you to go out and take the dog with you, that's what I told you, I didn't tell you to kill the puppy by dragging him," she said to him.

And then
"Set snares for rabbits a little ways out there!" she told him.
He went and set snares up in the spruce trees, and all the little birds got caught and were hanging there.
They died.

Ay eł
diitsǫǫ haniiyilshyah.
“Jan iin ch’a hudhihtlǫǫ iin,” diitsǫǫ ehnih.
“Tsugaay iin xa dach’įįtl’u <<laa>> ndihnih ha, gah kah dach’įįtl’u
ndihnay,”
utsǫǫ yehnih.

Eł xǫǫshyąą, t’oo ch’a dąy
nts’ą’ shtutni’ xale’ dąy’.

Do::gn staniishyah dą’
do::gn dahtsaah da’ee’ąą
tl’aan iket shi’ eł neetsay shi’
diniign
<eł> udzih shi’ gah tah ik’it danetdog.
“Ishyiit nts’ą’ tsuunaa,” diitsǫǫ ehnih.
“<Ena’>,” utsǫǫ yehnih.

Ay eł
etsaa:: shits’ą’ tsuunaa xa.
Dineh choh t’oot’eey etsaa.
Yaa ishyiit nihniinaan eł hanoog kon’ utsǫǫ dehk’an.
Ts’oo shyah hohuhtsiin shyiit dihdeltth’ix.
Daxat ts’oo nitdee’aay ettheeł ettheeł.
“Ena’ ndihnih! Neek’it tatnaaxüü, ndihnih,” utsǫǫ yehnih t’oot’eey
hǫǫt’eey yettheeł eł t’axoh
t’axoh ishyiit
tay’ neettheel eł nahdǫǫ nahal’uuk nts’ą’ diniign
neetsay
<eł> udzih gah taatna’įįtl’įįt.
Huushi’ ntl’aa::n hah’ogn.

Oh! Xǫǫshyąą t’oo łaan dįįdąy.

And then
he brought them back to his grandmother.
"This is what I caught in the snares," he told his grandmother.
"I didn't tell you to set snares for birds, I told you to set snares for
rabbits,"
his grandmother told him.

He was smart, but he still did this,
to see what she was going to say to him.

He went away a long way
he put up a cache way up there
and in it, meat, bear meat,
moose
and caribou meat, and rabbit, he piled in it.
"Let's move there," he said to his grandmother.
"No," his grandmother told him.

And then
he cried, so they would move there.
He was a big man, but he cried.
They all moved there and his grandmother made fire.
They made a spruce house and stayed in it.
He was chopping and chopping at the spruce that was standing there.
"No, I'm telling you, it'll fall on us, I'm telling you," his grandmother
said to him, but he just kept chopping and enough,
enough, there
he kept chopping and it all fell down and the moose,
the bear
and the caribou and rabbit meat spilled over.
They had lots of food out there.

Oh! He's smart, but he still does that.

“Shin du’ tsǫǫniiniign nudihnih,” utsǫǫ yehnih.
“Nts’ą’ shdinih nts’ą’ shkah nihtah de’ kah ch’ale hǫǫ naa dihdąy.”
K’at’eey hǫǫsu’ iik’ah nehtah de’, <<nts’ą’ utaaniɫ le’>>.

Teejuh yuunih nts’ą’ iik’ah nehtah.
Ch’its’ąą tah daada’an tah.
<<K’at’eey hǫǫsu’ dąy t’oot’eey utsǫǫ hǫǫsu’ iik’ah nehtah.>>

<<Nadelsüü iin>> hiixa edloo:.
Ay ts’iiniin, “Nuh’ich’oo nak’įįɫ nts’ą’ dihdį’” nts’ą’ hunaanich’ehthad nts’ą’ niithan.

Ay eɫ aayh
aayh chih <eedlah>
aayh ishyiit
shyüh shyiit ishyiit natetdagn ha.
Ay mbee’eh
diniign kah
udzih kah teedeel eɫ.
Diit’ah huda’ huuk’eh
huunaatagn nts’ą’ huuk’eh teltthat
eɫ anoo’
haadal.

Nedzeegn <udzih ntl’aan tah niishyah>
udzih iineh’įį.
Dii’aayy’ tthiiteettheet *way out*.
Hiik’eh teetshyaaɫ nts’ą’
noo::’ nts’ą’
aayh eɫ
teltthat udzih nts’ą’
udzih ha įįxąą hǫǫ ntl’aan t’eey.

"I thought you were not smart," his grandmother told him.
"I did all this to see how you cared for me, what you would say."
Had she not taken good care of him, I don't know what would have happened.
She took pity on him[1] and she took care of him.
He did things the wrong way.
He didn't do things right, but his grandmother took good care of him.

The hunters laughed at him.
And the child thought, "I will show you what I can do."

And snowshoes
he had snowshoes too
snowshoes, there
and he was walking in the snow.
And his maternal uncle
for moose
and for caribou they went.
He, after them
he ran after them
way up there
they were walking.

Nedzeegn ran into lots of caribou
he saw caribou.
He threw his snowshoe far away.
He jumped as far as he could toward them and
way out
with the snowshoes
he ran toward the caribou
he killed lots of caribou.

Ay eł
“Udzih
“<łahtthagn> nts’ą’ udzih ay didhagdak stach’idzineedlah udzih.”
na’inshyay eł nih.
Hiihohnii’inshyah.
Hiidehtsii.
<Łahtth’agn> nts’ą’ hiints’ą’ ts’ani’elt’eh.
“Nedzeegn
“udzih iin ch’a stach’idzineedlah iin
“k’at’eey nahiitsaldaa,” hiiyehnih.

Ishyiit nts’ą’:
“Anat! Shints’ą’ ahdał!
“Ishyiit dą’ deltth’ih!” huu’ehnih.
Naa chih nts’ą’ hihteedeeł udzih <łahtthagn nts’ą’> įįdlah nts’ą’
ha’įįhxąą.
Udzih iin <łahtthagn nts’ą’> huugn hįįłaag <łahtthagn nts’ą’> hiidaltsįį.
Hǫǫ shįį t’eey.

Ch’inoht’iin
ay xa etsaa: eł
k’at’eey hiitl’aa yehchuudn.
Ch’anii’eltsanh dą’ chih dineh tl’aahiiyetįį,
k’at’eey dą’ ts’iiniin tl’aa yehchuul k’at’eey.
Etsaa: nts’ą’ t’eey degn tah.
Ch’aldzeeg shyiit nts’ą’ tah teeshyah.
Aadeg ch’aldzeeg shyiit ch’ale na’ethadn hǫǫt’eey
ch’aldzeeg nah’įį de’.

Hǫǫsǫǫ ts’ąy
diiła’ eł
ch’inohtįį uut’on <nts’ą’>
tl’ah ts’ąy ch’iiła’ du’
dii le’ ła a’aal

And then
The caribou
"I [shot and] missed all the caribou and the caribou ran away,"
he told them when he came back.
He came back near them.
They cussed at him.
They were all mad at him.
"Nedzeegn
"the caribou ran away from him,
"we will not forget this for you," they said.

And then:
"Over there! You guys go after me!
"They're still over there," he said to them.
They all went where all the caribou were lying around, killed.

All the caribou were dead and they were scattered all over.
That's it.

Sausage
and he was crying
[because] they didn't give it to him.
They gave it to a stingy man,
they didn't give it to the child.
He cried and he went up
He went away, up into the moon.
He's standing up in the moon
when you look at the moon.

On the right side,
with his hand
he is holding the moose stomach and
in his left hand
they don't know what he's holding

ay eł uxol du' <ts'ehłagn>
uxol du' degn
tah
hiiyuteneegn k'at'eey hiiyuunagn eł hǫǫt'eey uxol nt'eh.
Ts'ehkah t'eey ay ch'aldzeeg shyii dineh gaay eeday nah'įįł.
Any time of night or when you look at the moon, you can see that boy is still up there.

It's a sad story, that one.

and one leg
that leg up
there
they tried to grab him and couldn't catch him so he jerked his leg up.
You can plainly see that boy up there in the moon.
Any time of night or when you look at the moon, you can see that boy
is still up there.

It's a sad story, that one.

Transcribed and translated with the help of Avis and Roy Sam.

Notes

1. Literally: someone had mercy on them.

15

Yamaagn Teeshyaay xa nahogndak

Jan ch'a
Jǫǫ eł Chįhttheel eł
hanats'iholnak niign.

Jǫǫ dishyįį'
hah'ogn eedah
eł
Yamaagn Teeshyaay huuts'ą' aahaał eł.
Uhaniishyah,
Chįhttheel eł.

<<Ay tl'aan>> Yamaagn Teeshyaay,
"<Dihtsįį!>
Dihtsįį!" <nih>.

15

I talk about Yamaagn Teeshyaay

This story, and the two that follow it, are part of the story cycle about Yamaagn Teeshyaay, 'he who went around [the world]'. During his travels, Yamaagn Teeshyaay encounters many different people, human and animal. In many cases, Yamaagn Teeshyaay is responsible for the animals' appearance and behavior.

This story was told in two parts on the same day.

This is
Camprobber and Woodpecker
a story we tell about them.

Camprobber, all alone,
was sitting out there,
and
Yamaagn Teeshyaay walked up to them.
He came to their camp,
with Woodpecker.

And Yamaagn Teeshyaay,
"I'm hungry!
"I'm hungry!" he said.

<Ay tl'aan>
Jǫǫ:
"Chįhttheel,
hah'ogn,
dii įį'aal mbatl'a įįkaayh," yehnih.
Chįhttheel eł kee aadogn
dahtsaa da'ee'an shyiit nts'ą'
gǫǫh, tsat
tsat gų'
yaa ninįįkąą <nts'ą'>.

Jǫǫ ts'aani'elt'eeh eł.
Jan du': "Ayah! Dii xa dįh'ąąy?" yehni.
Eł
"Ayshyįį dii xa ch'ih'aal le'," Chįhttheel hiiyehnih.
"Ayah!"
Jǫǫ dii yihchuut tl'aan nit'aayįhtl'iit nts'ą' jah dugn.
"Gǫǫh t'ayaadn.
"Dineh k'a t'eey itgha'aal, ndee ch'a dįį'ąąy?" yehnih.

This segment was inserted later the same day:

Jǫǫ <eł> Chįhttheel eł łihetxąą eł.
Łihtetxąą eł.
Jǫǫ tthi'
kon' shyiit nįįshyil eł
Jǫǫ hatniik'ąą nts'ą' utthi'
<łahtthagn nts'ą'> delgayh.
Ay tl'aan eł Chįhttheel
unii tl'aan iiche' ts'ąy tiithal idihshyiil eł uche' <łahtthagn nts'ą'>
hadeek'ąąn nts'ą'.
Uche' chįį <łahtthagn> nts'ą' t'eey hadiik'aan eł delgayh nłįį.
Hǫǫt'eey heltsįį.
K'ahdu' t'eey

And then
Camprobber:
"Woodpecker,
out there,
bring him what you eat," he said to him.
And Woodpecker up there
there is a cache and inside
worms, wood
wood worms
he brought them in a bowl to him.

Camprobber got mad.
That one: "Yuck! Why do you do this?" he said to him.
And
"This is all I ever eat!" Woodpecker said to them.
"Yuck!"
Camprobber grabbed [the worms] and dumped it all out.
"Worms are not good to eat.
"A man can't eat this, why do you bring this?" he said to him.

This segment was inserted later the same day:

Camprobber and Woodpecker were fighting.
They started to fight.
Camprobber's head
he shoved it in the fire and
and Camprobber got burned and his head
it became white all over.
And then Woodpecker
grabbed him and pushed his butt, tail forward, into the fire, and the tip of his tail burned.
The tip of his tail burned up and became white.
They still look that way.
Even today,

hǫǫt'eey heltsįį.
Utthi' adihk'ąąn tl'aan iiche' chįį' tadehkąąn hǫǫt'eey naant'i.

End of inserted segment.

Ay eł
Jǫǫ:
"The'!
"Aadog dahtsaa shyiit
"unok'įį."
Jǫǫ aadog dahtsaa shyiit nts'ą' <<Yamaagn>> Teeshyaay
mba' eł
jign utah xee
dinayh utah xee
yaa ni'inkąą.

Eł
Yamaagn Teeshyaay iycldeeł:
"Jan ch'a nsǫǫ!" Yamaagn Teeshaay: "Shaa elkąyh.
Hǫǫsu' t'eey ay nach'ih'aal; ts'inaa'iin," <nih>.

they still look that way.
His head burned, and the tip of his tail burned, and they still look that way.

End of inserted segment.

And then
Camprobber:
"Wait!
"Up there in the cache
"I will look for [something to eat]."
Camprobber [went] up into the cache and Yamaagn Teeshyaay
dry fish and
blueberries mixed with grease
bearberries mixed with grease
he brought in a bowl for him.

And
Yamaagn Teeshyaay ate it:
"This is good!" Yamaagn Teeshyaay: "This tastes nice.
I'm eating really well, thank you!" he said.

Transcribed and translated with the help of Cora David.

16

Yamaagn Teeshyaay Nahtsįą xa nahogndak

Nahtsįą ts'antleeg.

Nahtsįąh,
Yamaagn Teeshyaay yaa neeshyay eł,
"Hǫǫsu' nts'ą' dineh hǫǫłe' dii xa ch'a?
"Ts'adn nts'ą' hǫǫt'eh nts'ą' shįį' ts'ani'ilt'eh nts'ą'? K'a t'eey įsuuy!"
iyehnih.
Nahtsįą:
"Nxaa! Teladihdį' ha' nk'eh la dihdįį ay shiin xa' ch'a!

"Shk'eh
"nts'ą' dihdį' ni <ch'a> shk'eh ch'a dihdąy
"ts'iikeey iin t'eey shk'eh taadiił."

<Nts'ą'> Nahtsįą,
Yamaagn Teeshyaay ts'ani'elt'aay eł yi.
Yaa nineeshyay eł.
Nahtsįą gaay iin iik'it ełüh etsan du'.

16

I talk about Yamaagn Teeshyaay and Wolverine

This appears to be one of the most frequently told segments of the Yamaagn Teeshyaay cycle.

Wolverine was no good.

Wolverine,
Yamaagn Teeshyaay came to him and,
"Why are you not a good person?
The way things are going, you always get mad? You are not a good person!" he said to him.
Wolverine:
"None of your business! You do it for yourself, I don't do this like you for myself!
Like me
how I do it, the way that I do it,
the children will do it like me."

And Wolverine,
Yamaagn Teeshyaay got mad.
He walked up to him.
The little wolverines, they peed and shat on top of him.

Yamaagn Teeshyaay ts'ani'elt'ee nts'ą', Nahtsįą haanineeshyah nts'ą'.
"Du noo' įįtthał!" nii t'eey.
"Nts'ą' ndihnih niitįįdiił.
"Shi' udįh'ąą de' ch'ihtįįtsah nts'ą' uk'it tįįłüh de' uk'it tįįtsąą nts'ą'.

"Tįįtsah.
"Huu'eeł shyiit t'eey staatilshyeek nts'ą' nii'įįł nts'ą' ay kįį tįįdaał,"

Nahtsįą ehnih.

Ay tl'aan eł Nahtsįą ts'ą' noo'teeshyah.

Yamaagn Teeshyaay got mad and he walked up to Wolverine, and:
"Run this way!" he said.
"You will do as I tell you.
"When you find meat, you will bury it and you will pee on it and shit on it.
"You will bury it.
"You will take home what is in their traps; you will steal it and you will live by that,"
he said to Wolverine.

And then he went back, away from Wolverine.

Transcribed and translated with the help of Rosa Brewer.

17

Yamaagn Teeshyaay Naadodi xa nahogndak

Neenaattheh dą' Yamaagn Teeshyaay
keey dą' nįįshyah.
K'at'eey huh dineh diltth'ii,
jee'aan diltth'ak.

Teetsaan ney dǫ dǫ dǫ,[1]
<henih>.

Ay eł Yamaagn Teeshyaay shyuugn nandetah ndee nts'ą' hǫǫnay.

Jah ch'aach'in'.
Ay neh'ąy eł ay eetał eł.

"Oh! Oh! Shk'įkaagn'![2]
"Shk'įkaagn'," nts'ą' hehnih.
Eł Yamaagn Teeshyaay ishyiit na'ehthat.
Ay eł t'eey Naadodi iin ha įį'üüt,
Naadodi iin du' "Dii xa neeshyah ghintal?" hiiyehnih.

⁓ 17 ⁓

Yamaagn Teeshaay and the Ant People

This seems to be a little-known part of the Yamaagn Teeshyaay story cycle.

Once upon a time, Yamaagn Teeshyaay
came to a village.
There were no people staying there,
[but] he heard singing.

Teetsaan ney dǫ dǫ dǫ,
they say.

And Yamaagn Teeshyaay looked around to see where the sound was coming from.
There was a tree stump.
He saw it and he kicked it.

"Oh, oh! My pack!
"My pack," they were saying.
And Yamaagn Teeshyaay was standing there.
And then all the Ant people crawled out of there,
and the Ant people said to him, "Why did you kick our house?"

"Ndee nts'ą' jee'an ay ha ch'ale ishyiit ch'aach'in' dhihtal," huu'ehnih.

"An!"
"Jah
"ashyuugn ch'il tatts'iłe' ha nee'eł dhindah," hiiyehnih.[3]

Ay eł hashyuugn eedah.
Nchaa nts'ą' k'at'eey huushyah dą' ihhaay.
Eł ch'ithüh guuy eł hiitl'a' į̨dlah.
"Jan ch'a naats'ehotį̨l," hiiyehnih.
"Shiign ts'ihotį̨ł dą' ch'ale daniishyay," hiiyehnih.
Ay eł
Yamaagn Teeshyaay dlok yinihthanh,
edloh huuxa.
Dii guu::y ch'itüh
nts'ą' dok'į̨ ha ch'ihtl'ahį̨yį̨dlay eł niithan eł?
Yaa edloh.

Ayshyį̨' t'eey t'axoh
Yamaagn Teeshyaay Naadodi iin haneeshyay Naadodi į̨łį̨.

Notes

1. Ants have their own language. The last three words indicate the beating of the drum.
2. Cora translates this word with "my pack" (this is another instance of the Ant language) and explains that the Ant people are talking about their eggs that they carry about.
3. The Ant people tell him that they are holding a potlatch and that they would like him to join them, so they can give him a gift, too.

"I didn't know where the song was coming from, so I kicked the stump," he said to them.
"Come!
"There
"we're distributing cloths among people, come sit with us," they said to him.

And he sat down on the ground.
He's so tall that he can't go into their house.
And they give him a little piece of moose hide.
"This is our potlatch gift to you," they said to him.
"We were making potlatch, when you came in," they said to him.
And
Yamaagn Teeshyaay smiled just a little bit,
he laughed for them.
This little skin,
he thought, what am I going to do with it?
He laughed about it.

This is the end.
This was the story about how Yamaagn Teeshyaay came to the Ant people, they were Ant people.

Transcribed and translated with the help of Cora David.

Cora’s uncle Charlie Mason

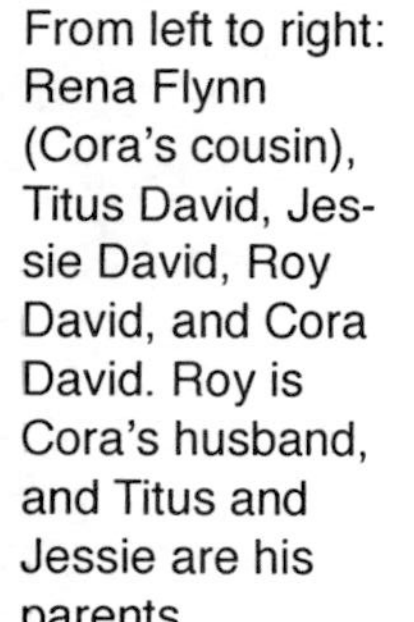

From left to right: Rena Flynn (Cora's cousin), Titus David, Jessie David, Roy David, and Cora David. Roy is Cora's husband, and Titus and Jessie are his parents.

18

Stsǫǫ Kelahdzeey xa nahoholndag

Neenaattheh dą'
ts'exeh gaay
łaakeey iin
hihdelxoo:: hah'ogn.
Laalil nahneedak.

Laalil huuch'a natnet'aay nahiitneedak eł
huunaa huuts'ą' ehsał nts'ą': "Ena'! Sǫ'!
"Laalil natnatdagn
staanuhtaałeeł nt'eh,"
huu'ehnih.
T'oot'eey k'at'eey hiidiitth'agn nts'ą'
laalil nahdogn ch'idanh keey k'etah kehuu'iidlah.
Eł huu'ihhuushyaak.

~ 18 ~

The story they tell about Grandmother Spider

This is a very common story in the Upper Tanana area. The story emphasizes the importance of living a good life by following the narrow (difficult) trail.

Special thanks go to Rosa Brewer, who not only helped transcribe a large portion of this story, but also pointed out that a part was missing. That part was recorded later and has been inserted.

Once upon a time
girls,
two,
were playing outside.
They were following a butterfly.

The butterfly was flying away from them; they were following and
their mother hollered at them: "No! Don't!
"If you follow the butterfly,
he'll take you away,"
she said to them.
But they didn't listen and
the butterfly took them to a different village.
And they got lost.

<Ay tl'aan>
Ts'igąągn
Ts'igąągn gaay huuxa da'eedah de'.
Tąy hǫǫts'eeg eł tąy teeł eł hǫǫłįį dą', Ts'igąąk da'eedah.
Ts'igąąk:
"Nduu tidhahdeeł ch'a dahdąy?" hu'ehnih.
"Nee'ihhuushyaak nduu tsudeel k'a hits'itnay," hinih.
Ay eł
Ts'igąąk: "Tąy ts'eegn k'i ahdeeł, sǫ' tąy teeł k'i ahdeel!" huu'ehnih.

Ch'aadeh du'
didia' tąy ts'eeg tąy choh k'i įhtįį.
Negn tah teedeeł k'a tąy ts'eeg k'i hiidal.

Ndegn hteedeel eł t'eey
ch'itay
ch'itay dishyįį' eeday ha hihnįįdeeł.
Ts'ant'ay łan,
<hinih>.

Ishyiit dą' hihnįįdeel eł.
Tiihatna::k.
Hihdįtsįį:: eł.
"Nuhxa
"tuuthał oktsąy," hu'ehnih.
"Hą'."
"Ayt'oo, dįįtsįį nats'u'aal," hinih.
Ay eł tuuthał hutl'aa įįkąą.
Ch'idia' hashiign tuuthał shyiit huneh'ąy eł
łiign naagn' dii naagn' le' ushyiit natatdiiłek.

And then
Chickadee
little Chickadee was sitting there for them.
There was a narrow trail and a wide trail, where Chickadee was sitting.
Chickadee:
"Do you know where are you going?" he said to them.
"We're lost, we don't know which way to go," they said.
And then
Chickadee: "Go onto the narrow trail, don't go onto the wide trail!" he said to them.
The older sister
took her younger sister to the wide, big trail.
They started walking that way, they didn't go on the wide trail.

They started walking that way and
an old man
they come to an old man, staying all by himself.
Devil truly,
they call him.

They came there.
They were tired.
They were hungry.
"For you
"I will make soup," he said to them.
"You guys."
"It's OK, we'll eat [because] we're hungry," they say.
He gave them soup.
The younger sister looked into the soup and
there were dog eyes, or eyes of I don't know what moving around in there.

Eł:
"K'at'eey tih'aal!" yuunih nts'ą'
dushyiign t'eey naatehtl'iit dą' ch'itay nahtak.
Ch'aadeh du' naye'aał.

Nateexeel eł
ch'aadeh <<eł>>
didia' hu'
hehtiat.

<Łahtthagn> nts'ą' diits'a' <hįįdląą> nts'ą' yineh'įh eł ch'idia'.
Ch'itay
ch'iitsay nihthiił tl'aan nih kon' nia' tthiidįįtthayh nts'ą'
delt'al de' eltsiin eł
yaadeh shyiit
yeł
ushyiit diyįtthay eł.
Maadeh ehtįį.
<Łahtthagn nts'ą'> yineh'įįh.

Nts'ą' dį' nts'ą' t'eey eł k'ahmann' eł, ts'iniithat nts'ą'.
Nah'ogn ti'uhshyah.
Ch'itay: "Dii xa ch'a titįhaał?" iyehnih.
"Jah shįįtl'aat t'eey,
"shįįtl'aat t'eey ni'įįha'," iyehnih.
"<Ena'>,
"k'at'eey hǫǫtihdil,
"aya'.
"Nah'an ti'uhshyah!"
Ch'ithüh tl'uul iitl'adn niniidlah tl'aan nah'an tinehtįį.
Nee ał shyiit įįshyaay eł.

Ch'aachin' dą' ishyiit dą' ch'aachin' iin t'eey hǫǫ hǫndąy.
Ch'aachin'

And:
"I'm not going to eat this!" she thought and
she spilled the soup when the old man wasn't looking.
The older sister ate it.

It got dark and
the older sister and
her younger sister
slept.

Everything, the younger sister was looking.
The old man
put steel in the fire to make it very hot
until it looked red and
into the older sister
with it
he pushed it into her.
Her older sister died.
She saw it all.

And the next morning, she woke up early.
She wanted to go out.
The devil said to her, "Why do you want to go out?"
"In my hands
"you can go to the toilet here in my hands," he said to her.
"No,
"I won't do that,
"it's yucky.
"I want to go out!"
He tied a skin rope around her and she went outside.
She went to a clump of bushes.

Tree stumps, long time ago, the tree stumps even were alive.
Tree stump,

"Dą' tl'uuł nǫǫłeek de'," Ch'aachin' ehnih.
"Ishyiit dhihda k'eh tl'uuł nǫǫłeek de'," ay ts'exeh gaay du' teltthat.
Noo::' shyiit altthał nts'ą'.

This bit was inserted on August 11, 2009.

Haniig choh ts'exeh ni'iltthat.
Ts'ant'ay ch'a eł.
Ishyiit huu Noogaay shįį' natetdaak haniig choh t'ah
yaa ni'iltthadn eł
"Naann' ske'uhshya' nts'ą' łaan?
"Nche' k'it de' sketihhaał hǫǫłįį t'oot'eey nts'ą' iynįįthan," yehnih.

Ay eł
Noogaay,
"Huh dii natįįłeek de' ay eł shihǫǫkeet de' naann' skentakteeł," yehnih.

"Tsayh shįį' jah natihłeek.
"Huh dii tsayh eł nnidhihtsayh eł dįltthox tiiltsayh."
Ay eł Noogaay du' "Duka' hǫǫshįįłeeł tl'aan naann' skentakteeł,"
<<yehnih>>.
Naann' diiche' yaa sketnįtthay k'it skeneeshyah.
Neljiit! Ts'exeh neljiit nts'ą', "Hanteey!" iyehnih t'oot'eey

Noogaay du' natateehthak.
Ay eł
"Hanteey!" yehnih.
Iiche' k'it naann' skeneeshyah nts'ą' naann' tah hunaann' tah sta'iltthat.

End of inserted segment.

Ay naattheh du'
ch'iithoo <eł>

she said to the Tree stump, "Bring that rope back around it!
Wiggle the rope as if I was there," and that girl started to run.
She kept running far that way.

This bit was inserted on August 11, 2009.

The girl came running to a big river.
The devil [right behind her].
Fox was walking around by himself at the edge of the big river,
she ran to him and
"I wonder how would I cross the river?
I can easily go on your tail but what do you think about that," she said to him.

And then
Fox:
If you pay me with whatever you carry, I'll take you across," he said to her.
"Ochre is the only thing I can offer to you.
"If I paint you with this ochre, then you will turn orange."
And Fox, "Go ahead, paint me, and then I'll take you across," he said to her.
He put his tail across [the river] and she crossed on it.
She was scared! The girl was scared and "Hurry up!" she said to him but
Fox was taking his time.
And
"Hurry up!" she said to him.
She crossed over on his tail and then she ran away.

End of inserted segment.

And long time ago
a scraper

mbeetsal <eł>
nahuugn tthee dii'eł dii'eedlah <chih>.
Hiitl'aa hiiyįįdląy.
"Jan manh uułe'," nih dik'eetl'aat nts'ą' yidehnay.
Tthiiteet-tthak tah manh cho::h eltsiik.
Ay tl'aan "Jan ddhał uułe'!" niik tah ddhał cho:h eltsiik.

<Nts'ą'> ch'itay
ts'exeh k'eh alttha::ł.
<Nts'ą'>
manh cho:h maagn nii'eltthał tah, hiimaagn ts'ak tiiteltthak dą'.
Dziin t'eey meł hǫǫłeek.
Tl'aan ddhał choh tachih ddhał tüh niithaadn t'eey hǫǫłeek nts'ą'.
K'at'eey yaa na'ehhaay.

Altthał diinah
Kelahdzeey
Kelahdzeey iin haanoogn shyah łaan hah'ogn nts'ą' hudehgod eł.
"Doo ch'atnąy?"
Kelahdzeey iiyehnih.
"Shin! Shin.
"Tsǫǫ, shin diht'eh," nih.
Tsǫǫ,
"Daniihaay!" yehni.
"K'at'eey nkah hutnak'įįl, daniihaay.
"Nnak'įh de', ntth'an natal'oh," yehnih.

Ay eł
daniishyah tl'aan
"Adaat
"ch'ithüh,
"ch'ithüh ts'an ay shyiit iltthiit!"
yehnih.

a fish knife
and also some rocks, she had with her.
She throws them behind her.
"There shall be a lake!" and threw it behind her.
and it became a big lake.
And then: "This shall be a mountain!" she said and there was a big
mountain.

And the old man
kept running after the girl.
And
when he came to the shore of the lake, he ran around the lake.
It took him all day.
He walked across the mountain; it's a long way.
He didn't catch up with her.

She ran and there was
Spider
the house of the Spider people, and she knocked on the door.
"Who is that?"
the Spider said to her.
"Me, me!
"Grandma, it's me!" she said.
The grandmother,
"Come in!"she said to her.
"I'm not going to look at you, come in.
"If I look at you, your bones will fall off you," she said.

And then
she went inside and
"Over there
"skin bag
"run inside the skin bag!"
she said to her.

Ay shyiit iinshyah tl'aan chinel'įį
eł nah'ǫǫ nts'ą' eł
hudeldonh eł
"Daniihaayh!" yehnih.

The devil ran right behind that girl.
"Mmm huhuhuhu," <nih>.
Edloo nts'ą'
"Nday jah ts'exeh njah duu nts'ą' t'eey utsįį huni'elt'ay ha, jah nts'ą' ay tidhihshyah," nih.
Ch'itay eł shuugn uneh'ąy eł
Kelahdzeey ts'ist'e',
"An staaniida'!
"Nts'ą' hajaktthak nts'ą' ntth'an nataadah," yehnih.

Ch'itay du', "K'at'eey staatihdal!
"Jah t'eey tihdal," nih.
Ay eł
Kelahdzeey ts'ist'e' iikah huneh'ąy eł utth'an <łahtthagn nts'ą'> nateetdeek.

"An, an an! Tiniltthit ha eltthiit jah jan ay uułe' diinih," yehnih.

"Jan jign uułe' jan tsüü uułe',
"jan ntl'at uułe' <łahtthagn nts'ą'> jah nan' k'it dii eedlah nts'ą' ay ǫǫłe' de'," iiyehnih.
Ay eł ch'a nah'ogn jign ehtah
nishyeey nts'ą'
tsüü tah ts'eldeel nishyeey hǫǫłįį.

Ay eł t'axoh eł
ushüü <taagn> iin nahatdał.
Ts'exeh gaay
hahnoogn

She went into [the bag] and hid
and outside
there was a knock and
"Come on in!" she said.

The devil ran right behind that girl.
"Mmm huhuhuhu," he said.
He was laughing and
"I followed the scent of the girl here, that's why I came here," he said.

The old man looked around and
old lady Spider,
"Quick, go away!
"I will turn around and look at you and your bones will fall down," she said to him.
The devil, "I won't go away!
"I will stay right here!" he said.
And then
old lady Spider just looked at him and all his bones fell down.

"Quick, quick, quick! Run out, get out of that bag <grab a bone> and say what it'll become!" she said to her.
"These will be blueberries and this will be wild potato,[1]
"this will be cranberries and whatever grows here, that is what you're going to be," she said to [the bones].
And then out there berries
grew and
and wild potato and other edible plants were growing.

And then
her three sons came back.
The girl
right in the dwelling

huuts'adn shyiit yeedah.
Dahugn
nahugn huuts'ade shyiit ishyii yetdlag shyiit hǫǫhneh'ąy eł.
<Ch'etl'aa tay> ts'exeh gaay ishyii eedah.
"Shin sh'aat taałeeł, shin sh'aat taałeeł," henih.

Hǫǫ Kelahdzeey du' <nih>,
"K'a nuh'aa taałeeł eł
"dii xa dahnay," huu'ehnih.

Ts'exeh gaay: "Shnaa iin k'e ts'ehokdąą:y natuhshya',
"shnaa iin."
Ay eł tsǫǫ Kelahdzeey,
tthee cho::h stadįį'aan naan' hich'inihthat "Shiign hǫǫnih'įį!" eł
shiign uneh'ąy eł,
"Oh, shnaa iin! Shta' iin!" <yehnih>.
Ay eł,
"Tth'ee nįįdat,
"diniign thüh nįįdat yehni nts'ą' hǫǫdį' dziin."
Shii niyeh'aak.
Hahshiign nan' k'it k'at'eey hi'ihtǫǫ:: dį'.
T'axoh ishyiit k'eh
yinehtl'uul ninįį.
"Shiign t'axoh natonshyah," yehnih.

Natetshyay eł
nataadaal eł
"Sts'iikeey dineh iin nachihdheh'xįį de',
shuu kah tahshyüü:: nts'ą'
hugn ch'inłuut t'eey tahshyüü
hii'ǫǫndąyh de'," yehnih.
"Ahą."

she was in his bag [of one of the sons].
In there
they were looking in their bags.
The girl was in the last one.
"Me, she's going to be my wife, me, she's going to be my wife!" they
 said.
And that Spider said,
"She's not going to be you guys' wife,
"why do you guys say that," she said to them.

The girl: "I miss my parents, I want to go home,
"my parents."
And grandmother Spider,
she pushed the big rock cover aside with a stick and "Look down!" and
she looked down and,
"Oh, my mother, my father!" she said.
And then,
"Gather sinew,
make a rope out of moose skin during the day."
She measured it down [to see how far she had to go].
It didn't quite reach the ground below, so she kept on doing it.
Enough there
she tied enough rope.
"It's time for you to go down now," she said to her.

She went down and
after she left
"If my children kill me
it'll snow lots and
there will be hail and it'll snow
you will know by that," she said to her.
"Yes."

Shiign tah
nayį naałǫǫ'idihnąy eł *and*
dinaa iin naht'aagn t'eey nayįtįį.
"Oh! Shnaa! Shta'!" nih tah.
Dinaa iin dita' iin thiin huuniik.
Hin nahuunelts'ųų eł t'eey.

Tadn hǫǫłįį eł ehshyüü tl'aan ch'inłuut di ehshyüü.
"Oh!
"Stsǫǫ nahdhehxįį," nih.
Unaa iin uta' iin dii "Doo ch'a ntsǫǫ?" hiiyehnih.
"Kelahdzeey, stsǫǫ Kelahdzeey," nih.
"Nahdhehxįį kahol'įį," yehnih.
Shiign etsah.

Hǫǫ shįį t'eey.

Down
she let her down by the rope
she put her down right behind her parents.
“Oh, my mother! my father!” she said.
She hugged her mom and her dad.
She was kissing them again and again.

It became night and it started to snow and there was hail and snow.
“Oh!
“They killed grandma,” she said.
Her mother and her father, “Who is your grandmother?” they said to her.
“Spider, my grandmother Spider,” she said.
“This is a sign that they killed her,” she said to them.
She was crying right there.

That’s the end.

Transcribed and translated with the help of Rosa Brewer, Avis Sam, and Roy Sam.

Cora's maternal grandparents: Chief Luke from Copper Center and his wife, Helen.

Selected Bibliography

Resources on Upper Tanana and Tanacross

Arnold, Irene, Rick Thoman, and Gary Holton. 2009. *Tanacross Learners' Dictionary*. Fairbanks: Alaska Native Language Center.

Demit, Ellen, and David Joe. 2010. *The Adventures of Yaabaa Teeshaay: First Man Stories from Healy Lake as Told by Ellen Demit and David Joe*. Edited by Constance Ann Friend. Athabascan translated and transcribed by Irene L. Arnold and Richard Thoman. Fairbanks: Alaska Native Knowledge Network.

Guédon, Marie-Françoise. 1974. People of Tetlin why are you singing? National Museum of Man, Mercury Series, Ethnology Division, Paper no. 9. Ottawa

Guédon, Marie-Françoise. 1981. "Upper Tanana River Potlatch." In *Handbook of North American Indians. Vol. 6, Subarctic,* ed. June Helm, pp. 557–581. Washington, D.C.: Smithsonian Institution.

Holton, Gary. 2000. *The Phonology and Morphology of the Tanacross Athabaskan Language*. Ph.D. dissertation, University of California Santa Barbara.

Kari, James. 1997. Upper Tanana Place Names Lists and Maps. Compiled and edited by James Kari, Alaska Native Language Center. Final report for the project "Upper Tanana Athabaskan Place Names in the Vicinity of Wrangell-St. Elias National Park," sponsored by Wrangell-St. Elias National Park, during 1995–1997.

Kari, James M. n.d. *Upper Tanana Stem List*. Unpublished digital file. Ms. in the author's possession.

Kari, James M., and Olga Lovick (eds.). 2010. Upper Tanana Alphabet website. www.lithophile.com/olga/ut/alphabet.

McKennan, Robert A. 1959. The Upper Tanana Indians. *Yale University Publications in Anthropology,* No. 55. New Haven: Department of Anthropology, Yale University.

McKennan, Robert A. 1981. "Tanana." In *Handbook of North American Indians, Volume 6: Subarctic,* edited by June Helm, 562–576. Washington: Smithsonian Institution.

Milanowski, Paul G. 1961. Sound system of Upper Tanana Athapaskan (a preliminary view). In *Science in Alaska: Proceedings of the 12th Alaskan Science Conference*, 7–12. College, Alaska: Alaska Division, American Association for the Advancement of Science.

Milanowski, Paul G., and Alfred John. 1972. T'oodįht'aiy Aandeegn. PAUL Dinahtł'aa Ch'itheh eł Łaakeiy dan THESSALONICA Keiy' Koht'iin ts'ą' tł'aan Ch'itheh eł Łaakeiy dan TIMOTHY ts'ą' tł'aan TITUS ts'ą' tł'aan PHILEMON ts'ą' Neetł'at (God's Word. I and II Thessalonians, I and II Timothy, Titus, and Philemon: Upper Tanana and Today's English Version.) Fairbanks: Wycliffe Bible Translators.

Milanowski, Paul G., and Shirley David Jimerson. 1975. *Nee'aandeegn': Upper Tanana Dictionary*. Anchorage: Alaska Native Education Board.

Minoura, Nobukatsu. 1994. A comparative phonology of the Upper Tanana Athabaskan dialects. In Miyaoka, Osahito (ed.), *Languages of the North Pacific Rim* (*Hokkaido University Publications in Linguistics Number 7*), 159–196. Sapporo: Department of Linguistics, Faculty of Letters, Hokkaido University.

Tyone, Mary. 1996. *Ttheek'ädn Ut'iin Yaaniidą' Ǫǫnign': Old-Time Stories of the Scottie Creek People. Stories Told in Upper Tanana Athabaskan by Mary Tyone, Ts'ą' Yahnik.* Transcribed and edited by James Kari. Fairbanks: Alaska Native Language Center.

CPSIA information can be obtained at www.ICGtesting.com
Printed in the USA
LVOW080413270712
291728LV00002B/1/P